American Parties i

Roughly 65 years ago, a group of political scientists operating as the "Committee on Political Parties" of the American Political Association thought long and hard about whether the American parties were adequately serving their democracy, and made specific recommendations for improvements. Comparing the parties of this country to those of Great Britain, the Committee found the American parties to be lacking in such fundamentals as clear policy differences, strong and effective organization, and unity of purpose among each party's representatives in public offices.

Starting from that background, this book is intended to significantly enhance students' understanding of the American parties today by putting them in broader context. How do the twenty-first-century Democrats and Republicans compare to the APSA Committee's "responsible parties model" of the mid-twentieth? And how do the American parties compare to parties of other democracies around the world, including especially the British parties?

Harmel, Giebert, and Janda answer those questions and, in the process, demonstrate that the American parties have moved significantly in the direction of the responsible parties model, but while showing little inclination for implementing the greater discipline the Committee thought essential. Already having provided as much ideological choice as the British parties, the U.S. parties have now edged closer on the other critical requirement of legislative cohesion. The authors show that the latter has resulted "naturally" from the greater homogenization of the meaning of "Democrat" and "Republican" across the country, both within the electorate and now within Congress as well. The dramatic increase in cohesion is not the product of greater party discipline, but rather of sectoral realignments.

Robert Harmel is Professor of Political Science at Texas A&M University.

Matthew Giebert is a Ph.D. student in Political Science at Texas A&M University.

Kenneth Janda is Payson S. Wild Professor Emeritus of Political Science at Northwestern University.

This is a very well-written, concise, and surprising comparison between the American parties and those in the UK and other Western democracies. It demonstrates that the American parties in the mid-1900s were not as "irresponsible" as some have alleged, and that today's parties, while more "responsible," are not a natural fit with the current American political environment. Chapters end in great suggestions for student projects!

—**Marjorie Hershey,** *Indiana University*

In a sophisticated and highly original analysis, the authors apply the responsible party model to the political, social and cultural development of recent times. The results can be surprising. Indispensable for anyone wanting to understand the modern party system.

—**William Crotty,** *Northeastern University*

For decades, assessments of American political parties have been influenced by the norms and criticisms contained in the 1950 APSA report on Responsible Political Parties. This crisply-written book provides a valuable and often surprising reassessment of how American parties compare to parties in other nations and how much change has occurred since 1950.

—**Jeffrey M. Stonecash,** *Syracuse University*

In important respects, American political parties are more responsible now than ever before. Harmel, Giebert, and Janda show how we know this to be true in a compelling and accessible fashion. Their "be careful what you wish for" message is sure to provoke discussion in many classrooms.

—**Jeffrey D. Grynaviski,** *Wayne State University*

American Parties in Context

Comparative and Historical Analysis

Robert Harmel
Matthew Giebert
Kenneth Janda

Routledge
Taylor & Francis Group

NEW YORK AND LONDON

For support material associated with *American Parties in Context*, please go to www.routledge.com/products/9780415843683

Published 2016
by Routledge
711 Third Avenue, New York, NY 10017

and by Routledge
2 Park Square, Milton Park, Abingdon, Oxon, OX14 4RN

Routledge is an imprint of the Taylor & Francis Group, an informa business

© 2016 Taylor & Francis

The right of Robert Harmel, Matthew Giebert, and Kenneth Janda to be identified as authors of this work has been asserted by them in accordance with sections 77 and 78 of the Copyright, Designs and Patents Act 1988.

Library of Congress Cataloging in Publication Data
Names: Harmel, Robert, 1950– author. | Giebert, Matthew, author. | Janda, Kenneth, author.
Title: American parties in context : comparative and historical analysis / Robert Harmel, Matthew Giebert, Kenneth Janda.
Description: New York, NY : Routledge, 2016. | Includes bibliographical references and index.
Identifiers: LCCN 2015041079 (print) | LCCN 2015051471 (ebook) | ISBN 9780415843676 (hardback) | ISBN 9780415843683 (pbk.) | ISBN 9780203756089 (ebook)
Subjects: LCSH: Political parties—United States. | United States—Politics and government.
Classification: LCC JK2261 .H26 2016 (print) | LCC JK2261 (ebook) | DDC 324.273—dc23
LC record available at http://lccn.loc.gov/2015041079

ISBN: 978-0-415-84367-6 (hbk)
ISBN: 978-0-415-84368-3 (pbk)
ISBN: 978-0-203-75608-9 (ebk)

Typeset in Sabon
by Florence Production Ltd, Stoodleigh, Devon, UK

Printed and bound in the United States of America by Publishers Graphics, LLC on sustainably sourced paper.

Contents

Figures

Tables

Boxes

Preface

Roughly 65 years ago, a group of American political scientists[1] examined the British parties, liked what they saw (or at least thought they saw), and wrote a Report suggesting the potential benefits of transporting various features of the British-style parties to the United States. The British parties presumably conformed to a "responsible parties" model where each party (1) made very clear how its policy positions differed from those of its opponent(s) and (2) was cohesive enough to govern accordingly, such that voters would know all they needed to know to hold elected officials accountable simply by knowing their party affiliation. In the United States, on the other hand, the parties seemed to offer neither clear choices on the issues nor the ability to force their elected officials to abide by party promises, such that party labels served the electorate very poorly as a guide to actual behavior of individual elected officials in government. In order for the American parties to better serve their voters and their democracy more generally, they would need to reform themselves to be more like the British parties in organization (more capable), the internal exercise of power (more centralized), unity of purpose (more cohesive), and issue clarity (more of it).

Almost immediately after its publication, the so-called "Responsible Parties Report" became the subject of criticism, not the least because of its underlying assumption that the parties could, if only they wanted to, make the prescribed changes. While the Report acknowledged that the American parties operated in a system that differed from the United Kingdom in several important respects (e.g., presidential vs. parliamentary and federalism vs. unitary power), critics argued that too little recognition was given to the widely accepted argument that "parties are shaped by their environments." In an earlier study, we (Harmel and Janda 1982) specifically addressed that argument, and found that while party actors certainly have some say in the direction parties take, environments do indeed go far in shaping their parties.

In this book, we are guided by the APSA Committee's work in several regards. First, the Committee's major goals serve as an organizing principle for the book's chapters: ideological/issue clarity (Chapter 2), organizational complexity (Chapter 3), decentralization of power (Chapter 4), and legislative cohesion (Chapter 5). In the process, we effectively challenge each of the underlying assumptions: were the parties, at the time of the Committee's own work, as ill-organized, decentralized, incohesive, and lacking in issue clarity as the Committee assumed? Here, we rely heavily on material from Harmel and Janda's (1982) earlier study, placing the American parties in broadly ranging comparisons to parties of other democracies.[2]

Second, the Report serves as a meaningful historical reference point. The Committee recommended change in a number of specific directions; here, we take the opportunity to assess the extent to which those changes have been implemented. In the separate chapters that follow, we ask how well organized, how decentralized, how cohesive, and how clear the parties' policy differences are *today*, always within the context of how the parties looked in the 1950s and what the Committee recommended.

Third, we continue the Report's practice of comparing the American parties to their British counterparts, highlighting not only differences, but also ways in which the two systems' parties may have grown more alike over time. The comparison to the British parties is a natural one, not only because of the APSA Committee's past practice, but because the two countries share important features of political culture and electoral system, while differing in other important behavioral and institutional ways.

Throughout the book, we also take a tip from the Report's critics and ask not only the extent to which the parties had—at the time of the Report—been shaped by their environments, but also the extent to which any changes in the parties since then can be explained by changes in their environments as well. Indeed, it is possible that even if the American parties have become better equipped over time to fit the "responsible parties" model, this may have happened not so much because party actors sought to follow the Committee's recommendations, but rather because changes in their environment have pushed them in that direction.

In the last chapter of the book, we build on what we have learned in the previous objective-specific chapters—that the American parties have indeed become somewhat more distinctive and cohesive—and consider some broader implications of those changes for voting and for governing.

In addition to doing all of the above, each chapter also includes some suggested "exercises" and/or "projects" with which you can engage more directly in the research enterprise yourself. Appendices B and C at the end of the book consist of data and other information that will prove useful in doing those exercises and projects.

Notes

1 The Committee on Political Parties of the American Political Science Association was tasked to examine the parties and make recommendations for improvement (APSA 1950: ix).

2 For those familiar with Harmel and Janda's earlier study, we should note that while this book draws significantly from that publication, it is sufficiently different to be considered a new and distinct book. Though sharing a focus on comparison of today's parties to those at the time of the APSA Committee's work, there is even more emphasis here on explicit comparisons over time and space. Written 33 years after the earlier book, references to "current events" are obviously quite different, with less emphasis here on "party reform" and focus instead on today's controversies regarding the costs and benefits of moving closer to the APSA's model of parties, especially with regard to polarization. And of course, the interactive features of this book are entirely new.

Acknowledgments

The authors wish to thank our colleague at Texas A&M Jon Bond, three anonymous reviewers, and our acquisitions editor Michael Kerns for their helpful recommendations. Special acknowledgment goes to those graduate assistants and others whose effort contributed to the Part Change Project's issue position data; individuals are recognized on the Project's website. We also thank the American Political Science Association for granting permission to reprint the summary and conclusions from the Responsible Parties Report as Appendix A.

This book is dedicated to the students in our political parties classes, who were its inspiration.

1 Introduction

The Argument for More Responsible Parties

I think that a certain degree of polarization is healthy in a democracy. It clarifies choices people have in elections, and it helps voters to hold the parties accountable for their performance.

(Alan Abramowitz, cited in Rettig 2010)

For two centuries, thoughtful observers of American politics have debated the virtues vs. the drawbacks of political parties for representative governance. In the earliest days, even before the development of the first true party organizations, such important figures as George Washington and James Madison argued that parties would serve only to emphasize special interests to the detriment of the common good. Washington, for instance, warned in his farewell address that parties "serve to Organize faction, to give it an artificial and extraordinary force—to put in the place of the delegated will of the Nation, the will of a party; often a small but artful and enterprizing minority of the Community." Madison, in Federalist Number 10, equated "party" with "faction," which he defined as "a number of citizens, whether amounting to a majority or a minority of the whole, who are united and actuated by some common impulse of passion, or of interest, adversed to the rights of other citizens, or to the permanent and aggregate interests of the community." To Washington, the effect of parties was "baneful;" to Madison, factions caused "mischief."

Despite their concerns, however, such leaders recognized at the same time the inevitability of factionalism (or as they sometimes called it, "party spirit"). Washington wrote that the spirit of party "is inseparable from our nature, having its root in the strongest passions of the human mind" and Madison that "the latent causes of faction are . . . sewn in the nature of man." And thus, the project would be not so much how to keep parties from forming, but rather how to control their bad effects. Indeed, the framers witnessed—and to significant degrees participated in—the formation of the first modern political parties, the Federalists and the Jeffersonian Republicans, during the first few decades under the current Constitution.

The Legacy of the Framers

The parties that grew up on American soil, though, would continue to bear certain attributes that not only reflected the anti-party environment in which they were born, but also would set them apart from parties formed later in European democracies, including the United Kingdom. The first American parties were not, after all, the work of national-level political architects attempting to form well-oiled machines to spite the concerns of Washington and others. As noted by Joseph Charles in his treatise on the development of the American party system: "When we see the way in which the first popular party in the United States came into being, with its roots in Committees of Correspondence like those of Revolutionary times and its forms shaped by the local institutions of the middle states, we . . . see that it was a product of adjustment and growth, that it did not spring full-blown from the forehead of Jefferson or of anyone else." Having been formed initially from preexisting electoral committees at more local levels,[1] the American national parties would never be given the degree of control over their local organizations or even their elected officials that has traditionally been exercised by many parties (especially those on the left) of European democracies.

Although Washington was particularly concerned about "geographical" parties tearing the new country apart, and Madison was particularly concerned about the possible development of class-based parties, the reality is that the first American parties were in effect doing battle over a set of sometimes crosscutting interests (including religious, geographical, economic, and class-based). Unlike European "ideological" parties that developed later from social classes and movements, the American parties were and would remain more concerned over forging a successful electoral coalition than promoting a particular philosophy.

Washington and Madison and their peers were seemingly concerned over parties that would be so strong and cohesive internally—and so different from one another in their special interests—that good, fair, reasonable governance would be impossible to maintain without thoughtful vigilance and structural safeguards. That the parties that eventually developed here could ultimately be described as weak, incohesive, and non-programmatic might well have lessened the framers' concerns. But those very features would serve later to fuel a different set of concerns for another group of party thinkers: those who would actually come to favor stronger parties of the "European type."

The Argument for Stronger Parties

In the middle of the twentieth century, a group of American parties' scholars were commissioned by the American Political Science Association to take a thoughtful look at the American parties, assess their strengths and weaknesses in serving their country's democracy and citizenry, and prescribe solutions for the weaknesses. Upon concluding that the American parties were ill-equipped to serve either democracy or citizenry, the Committee on Political Parties looked to the British system, in particular, for solutions. Whereas the two major British parties offered clear programmatic choices to their voters, and could promise to discipline their elected officials who failed to live up to the party's promises, the American parties seemed ill-equipped to do either. How, the Committee wondered, could voters use party labels to hold officials accountable if (1) the parties failed to provide clear differences on the issues and (2) they lacked the tools for disciplining elected officials who ignored whatever promises their party did make? Those observations and arguments are found in one of the most oft-cited documents on the American parties: what is commonly referred to as the "Responsible Parties Report," first circulated in 1950.

In the Report, the Committee made a number of specific recommendations (see Table 1.1). Those that were most clearly and directly associated with the "responsible parties model" were: (1) build more effective party organization; (2) strengthen the national level of the party vis-à-vis its more local levels of organization; (3) clarify the programmatic differences between the two major parties; and (4) develop means of discipline so as to assure greater behavioral cohesion within each party.

With the end goal of providing voters with party labels that would be meaningful guides to how candidates would actually behave if elected into government, it seems obvious enough why it would be necessary to have (1) clear programmatic differences between the parties and (2) elected government officials who would stick with the parties' positions and not wander off on their own.

Less clear is why better organization and more centralized party power would be seen as so important. Indeed, those are better thought of as "necessary requisites" for the more obvious objectives. How, the Committee wondered, could party unity be accomplished without the threat of discipline—be it in removal of important committee assignments or in disfavor toward pet projects or whatever—and how could discipline be accomplished without significantly more power resting at the national level of the party? And how could the national level be powerful in the absence of substantially greater organization? After all, what they believed they saw in the American national parties was organizational weakness and lack of resources with which to effectively control their own business, much less control candidates and even state and local parties with the same name. The consequence of these weaknesses, it seemed to them, would be elected officials and local branches free to promote their own causes regardless of inconsistency with "the party's" wishes, with the end results of muddied messages and labels that signaled little about actual behavior in government.

Though the Committee never actually presented it in this way themselves, we might see in their prescriptions something of a road map for

Table 1.1 Detailed Recommendations of the APSA Committee*

Ideology

- Create Party Council to adopt and interpret platforms
- Platforms adopted every two years

Organization

- National Conventions held every two years
- Fewer delegates and alternates at national conventions
- Convention delegates apportioned by party strength in states
- National Committee maintains national party headquarters
- National Committee raises adequate funding
- Larger permanent professional staffs for national committees
- Candidate nominations made in closed primaries
- More pre-primary conventions

Decentralization

- National Convention more active in selection of National Committee members
- National Committee members reflect party strength of areas they represent
- Create Party Council to make recommendations about Congressional candidates
- Create Party Council to discipline state/local parties deserting national platform
- Require state platforms to be adopted after national platform
- State and local platforms made to conform to the national platform
- Adopt a national presidential primary

Cohesion

- Make platforms binding on all party officeholders at all levels
- Members of Congress to participate more actively in platform-writing
- Consolidate all House and Senate leadership positions into one committee
- Parties hold more frequent Congressional caucus/conference meetings
- Caucus/conference decisions on legislative policy are binding on Members of Congress
- No Committee Chairmanships by seniority for opponents of party programs
- Replace Rules Committee control of the legislative calendar with leadership control

---

* Table entries adopted/adapted from Ranney (1973) and Green and Herrnson (2002).

getting the parties from "where they were" to "where they would like them to be." Greater organizational complexity would be necessary for greater nationalization of party power, and the latter would be necessary for the discipline required to force greater cohesion, which—along with greater clarity of issue positions within each party and greater clarity of differences between them—would be necessary in order to make the party label a more useful tool for voters in deciding whom to support and in holding elected officials accountable.

Assuming the parties took the road map seriously, we might expect them to look quite different today from what the APSA Committee saw (or at least thought it saw) more than six decades ago.

The American Parties Today

In certain respects, the American parties do look quite different today from what the APSA Committee observed (or at least thought they observed) in the middle of the twentieth century. Few today would argue that the parties are so similar ideologically that it is difficult to tell them apart. And in an era when parties that appear to be internally united seem to oppose one another at every turn, regular "crossing of the aisle" to forge bipartisan coalitions seems a distant memory.[2] Extreme ideological polarization, rather than lack of partisan clarity, is by far the more common complaint today. Particularly in the context of divided government—when the presidency and at least one of the houses of Congress are controlled by different parties—viable threats of government shutdowns, defaulting on the national debt, and policy gridlock are at least partially the consequences of parties that are both more "programmatic" and more internally unified.

But did they get that way because they listened to the Committee and followed its road map? We will address each step in the road map in subsequent chapters, but for now we can say that in places, the parties clearly ignored the Committee's directions, and yet via alternative routes, they still drew closer to the desired endpoint. Even without a significant increase in the use of discipline, the parties have still achieved greater internal cohesion. And greater clarity of ideological differences between the parties has been accomplished largely without concerted efforts to make it happen. Instead of dutifully following a road map of prescribed steps, the American parties have become more programmatic and cohesive by more "natural" means, while not necessarily intending to do so.

In later pages of this book, we will find that while the American parties have indeed changed over time on some of the dimensions critical to the Committee's aspirations, it would be a significant exaggeration to suggest that they have fully achieved the Committee's ideal model. That model, of course, was based largely on their observations of parties in Great Britain, parties that were developed and that operated in a very different setting, not only physically, but also politically. Where Britain was a relatively small country, the United States was relatively large. Where British government was unitary, American government was "federal" (i.e., with multiple layers of significant authorities). And where British political powers were "unified" in a parliamentary system, America's were divided among separate branches of government (i.e., a presidential system). Those differences, which were certainly apparent to the Committee members in the 1940s and 1950s, are—to substantial degrees—still apparent today.

But to whatever extent the American parties have drawn closer to the British model, it would presumably be due—at least in significant part—to those contextual differences becoming either smaller and/or of less significance over time.

And in later pages—including in the next chapter—we will also find that the Committee may have unintentionally exaggerated some supposed differences between the two countries' parties, even as they looked at the time of the Committee's writing. In those instances, the *lack* of differences might—as we shall see—actually be explained by some important similarities between the United States and United Kingdom, with both being modernized societies with *similar* electoral systems and numbers of major parties.

Projects

Project 1.1: The Role of the Party Reformer

Party reformers, such as those who constituted the APSA Committee, must consider not only what they would like to see changed about the parties, but also what features they would like to see maintained.

Play the role of a party reformer (i.e., think of yourself as a member on a reform committee). What would be four things that you would want to change about the American parties? What would be four things that you would want to keep unchanged about the American parties?

Project 1.2: What Did a French Observer Say About Early American Political Parties?

French political philosopher Alexis de Tocqueville came to the United States in 1831 to observe and write about American society and politics. His observations and understandings were published in two volumes, in French, in 1835 and 1840. Both volumes are usually published together in English translations as *Democracy in America* and are regarded by scholars today as insightful commentaries on American politics. The complete text is available online as a PDF file.

In this book, we are regularly making comparisons between the parties most of us know best—the American parties—and the parties we know less about in other democracies. For de Tocqueville, the project was to bring his background in Europe to bear in learning more about American politics and parties. Outside observers can sometimes make mistakes while interpreting politics in contexts that are relatively new and "foreign" to them, but they can also generate important insights that "locals" may have missed. De Tocqueville wrote as a foreign observer of American parties in Volume 2, Chapter 2 of *Democracy in America*, titled "Of Parties in the United States" (pp. 279–288). After reading those 10 pages, write one page concerning something that de Tocqueville was either *dead right* or *dead wrong* about concerning party politics today.

Project 1.3: What Else Did Washington and Madison Say About Political Parties?

In the text above, we have quoted snippets about political parties by George Washington and James Madison. Read for yourself either Washington's 1796 *Farewell Address* or Madison's *Federalist Number 10* (1788) to see what else they had to say. Write no more than one page of text about either Washington's or Madison's observations on the role of parties (or factions) that seemed to you to be particularly insightful concerning party politics even today.

Both documents are readily available on the Internet.

Notes

1 See Charles (1961: 85).
2 Though each party still has its "moderate" and "more ideological" wings, it is more so the case today than in the recent past that the moderate wings of the parties do not significantly overlap and that the distance between the extremes within each party is smaller. At least in those senses, the parties are clearly more distinct from one another and at least appear to be more internally united. For example, "liberal Republicans" and "conservative Democrats" are mostly a thing of the past. In Congressional voting, this greater "internal party unity" is quite apparent, even though moderate/ideological splits within each party remain for other purposes. (Among the many others who agree with these points are Galston 2010 and Moss 2012.)

2 Ideology
How Different Are the Parties?

... the party appeals often sound much alike and thereby contribute
to the bewilderment of observers of American politics.

(V.O. Key, 1964: 220)

Introduction

When the APSA Committee wrote its Report in 1950, one of their longed-
for prescriptions for the American system was more "programmatic"
parties (i.e., parties offering a clear choice among clearly stated programs).
Such was already the case for the British parties (or so they thought), and
this was one of the features of the "responsible parties model" that should
be emulated in the United States. As they put it:

> Popular government in a nation of more than 150 million people
> requires political parties which provide the electorate with a proper
> range of choice between alternatives of action.

(APSA 1950: 15)

But what existed instead was a situation where the "alternatives between
the parties are defined so badly that it is often difficult to determine what
the election has decided even in the broadest terms" (APSA 1950: 3).
If the party labels are to act as meaningful surrogates for policy alternatives, they argued, and particularly if they are to facilitate rational voting,
then the parties must make clear what those labels stand for and that they
stand for things that are different between the parties.

But even if more "ideological" or "programmatic" parties were desirable, some doubted that such parties would actually be welcome within
a political environment that seemed better suited to "pragmatic" parties.
The American context seemed to lack all of the things that could make
it more receptive to programmatic parties: proportional elections (the
United States had the plurality form), a multiparty system (the United
States had just two major parties), and a sharp and deep ideological
division within society. The U.S. environment might require—and at least

---

Box 2.1 Programmatic vs. Pragmatic Parties

While American parties are normally described as "pragmatic" parties, the APSA Committee clearly considered the British parties to be more in line with the common conception of "programmatic" parties. The difference lies in the parties' relative commitments to "ideology" or issue/policy orientation as opposed to "power" or the winning of elections simply for the sake of gaining power. Candidates and elected officeholders from a programmatic party will presumably remain true to the party's ideological/policy program even when that may bring a cost in terms of reduction in public support. The pragmatic party's candidates and representatives will presumably be willing to change positions or policy commitments when that is deemed important for winning elections, thus abandoning "program" in favor of "power."

Some have pointed out that a given party may at times justify the "programmatic" label, while at other times deserve the "pragmatic" designation. Joel Paddock (2005: 95), for instance, argues that the American parties have transitioned from being pragmatic to more programmatic in recent times, due to party activists caring more about issues than they did in the past. Robert Leach et al. (2011: 96) argue that the British Conservative Party became less pragmatic and more programmatic due to the leadership of Margaret Thatcher in the 1980s, while the Labour Party became more pragmatic under Tony Blair in the 1990s.

---

would seemingly only reward—parties that were "pragmatic" rather than "ideological," with the result being just major parties that employed very similar and perhaps internally inconsistent approaches to issues if they hoped to win national elections.

In this chapter, we begin by "testing" the APSA Committee's basic assumption that the British parties provided distinct differences between their programs while the American parties did not, then consider how the Committee arrived at that assumption in the first place, and then address what would be necessary for the American parties to actually provide the greater "ideological distance" that the Committee preferred.

How to Compare Party Ideology

In order to systematically compare positions of political parties and the distance between those positions across a number of democracies, it is necessary first to develop a common "measuring stick" that has the same meaning across those cases, and in order to do that, we must first answer the question "choice of what?" In the case of parties' ideological positions, the most commonly accepted answer to "what" is on some ideological continuum. And in order to measure the distance between parties' positions on this ideological scale, we first must have a way of accurately placing the individual parties at positions along that scale.

For most, if not all, mature democracies in the world today, the ideological dimension that is most important in dividing voters into political parties is the "economic dimension" of politics, captured by the terms "left" and "right." On the left are found those parties that advocate a substantial role for government in the economic sphere, while on the right are found those parties that tend to advocate for a very limited role, if any, for government vis-à-vis the economy. As argued by Maurice Duverger (1972), this dimension of politics became dominant in Europe in the middle of the nineteenth century, as working-class parties of the left developed to advocate for governmental programs that would amount to a redistribution of wealth and hence a greater equalization of economic rewards. In reaction, parties on the right, supported by both the upper and middle classes, advocated for a hands-off (laissez-faire) approach. (See Box 2.2.)

Despite the more recent advent of issues that are claimed to fall on different ideological continua than the left-right scale, such as immigration and the environment, it can be argued that these issues still bear relevance to an economic dimension. Immigration concerns commonly relate to questions and concerns of unemployment, and environmental concerns play into questions of regulation. For example, parties of the left are more likely to accept and sponsor government action on confronting environmental issues, as government action is more ideologically acceptable for leftist parties than it is for parties of the right.

There are multiple ways by which to place political parties on the left-right continuum. One would be to ask party leaders where they would place the parties, another would be to ask voters where they would place the parties, while a third would be to ask political science experts where they would place the parties. To really know where the parties as organizations would place themselves, the most appropriate method would be to see what the parties' positions are on some common set of left-right "issues" in what has come to be seen as the single official statement of parties' policy positions in advance of elections; in other words, the election platforms (or "manifestos").

Our approach in this book is to identify the parties' positions on four different issues that political scientists would generally accept as different dimensions of left-right ideology, by using party platforms. The four issues are the scope of public welfare, redistribution of wealth (including progressive vs. regressive taxation), government role in economic decision-making, and control of the means of production.

Box 2.2 Left-Right vs. Liberal-Conservative

The terms "liberal and conservative" and "left and right" have been defined in many different ways across the literatures on politics and parties. In fact, in everyday discussion of politics in the United States, the terms "liberal and left" and "conservative and right" are often used interchangeably, as essentially synonymous.

We ourselves prefer a more "European" approach, explicitly distinguishing between the two pairs of terms, with each reflecting its own ideological dimension. To be more precise, we prefer the approach followed by French political scientist Maurice Duverger (1972).

By Duverger's historical account of ideological development in Western Europe, the first half of the nineteenth century was dominated by a political conflict between the "liberals" and "conservatives," over the issues of liberty, equality, and mass participation in politics. The growing middle class was already sharing in economic wealth, and now wanted to play more of a role in meaningful self-governance; the traditional aristocracy had grown accustomed to exclusive rights to political participation and was reluctant to share. But as the bourgeoisie (liberals) won their rights and liberties from the aristocracy (conservatives), that line of combat was replaced by a new set of issues emphasizing the economic struggle between workers and owners. This conflict would pit socialists (the left) seeking government guarantees of an end to the "exploitation of the worker" against capitalists (the right) decrying any governmental role in the economy as both unnatural and unwise.

For the time period of our own analyses as presented in this book, this "economic dimension of politics" was clearly the most relevant to party politics especially in Western European and Anglo-American democracies, and hence the reason we have focused on the left-right ideological cleavage for this chapter.

Two of the issues are component parts of the broader matter of whether government should play a role in "equalization of wealth." On the left are found those parties that advocate for a type of "governmental Robin Hood," collecting a disproportionate share of revenues from the rich and distributing a disproportionate share of benefits to the poor. On the right are found parties that advocate no role for the government in "equalization of wealth" and some parties whose policy positions might actually amount to some redistribution from poor to rich.

On the revenue side, left-wing parties are more likely, for instance, to advocate for tax mechanisms such as a "progressive income tax," which is designed to take a larger share of the income of the wealthy than of the poor for government use. This is done by assigning increasing tax rates for progressively wealthy citizens. In contrast, parties on the right would be more likely to advocate for "regressive" tax mechanisms such as sales taxes and "value-added" taxes. While such taxes would presumably apply the same rate to all purchases, whether by rich or by poor, they effectively result in taxing a larger share of the income of the poor, who tend to spend most of their income, than of the rich, who have the luxury of banking or investing larger shares of their income.

On the "benefits" side, parties of the left tend to advocate for an array of governmentally provided social welfare programs, such as "public assistance" for the poor, the aged, and the unemployed. Specific examples of such programs in the United States would include Social Security, Unemployment Insurance, Temporary Assistance for Needy Families (TANF), and the Children's Health Insurance Program (CHIP), as well as Medicare and Medicaid. In Great Britain, the list would also include the National Health Service (NHS). While some such programs are designed to cover the entire population, implicit in most is the desire to assist especially those who are in need. Parties of the right would tend to oppose extension of such programs and perhaps even favor a "rolling back" of existing programs.

The other left-right issues involve two possible types of direct government involvement within the economic sphere. On the left are found parties that prefer a strong and direct government hand in the economy, while on the right are parties favoring a "laissez-faire" (hands-off) approach.

Parties of the left, for instance, would advocate for a strong governmental role in making policies to prevent and/or control significant economic problems. To prevent the nation's economy from being struck with one or both plagues of runaway inflation or high unemployment, a left-oriented party would expect the government to develop and execute an array of monetary policies; in the event of such an economic plague, the government would be expected to develop effective solutions (e.g., the "wage and price controls" implemented by the Nixon Administration in the 1970s). Parties of the right would tend to oppose most or all government interference in the "natural development" of the economy. (See Box 2.3.)

Left-oriented parties would also favor a significant role for the government in the day-to-day functioning of the "means of production," whether indirectly through regulatory policies or directly by owning and operating the "means" themselves. The classic Marxist position, as represented in *The Communist Manifesto*, is that "The proletariat will use its political supremacy . . . to centralize all instruments of production in the hands of the state." Stopping short of advocating government ownership of *all* means of production, though, left-oriented parties may still prefer government rather than private ownership of major producers in the areas

Box 2.3 A Republican President and His "Leftist" Economic Policy

Government placing caps on how much wages and prices can increase over a given period of time?! Even as a temporary measure, there is no doubting that this is a leftist position, about as anti-rightwing as anyone could imagine. Yet in 1971 the government of the United States implemented wage and price controls in an attempt to rein in rising inflation. And it was not even a Democratic president who led the way; instead, it was Republican Richard Nixon! As recalled by Daniel Yergin and Joseph Stanislaw in their book *The Commanding Heights* (1997):

> While Nixon may have philosophically opposed intervention in the economy, philosophy took a rear seat to politics. He had lost very narrowly to John Kennedy in 1960 . . ." He attributed his defeat in the 1960 election largely to the recession of that year," wrote economist and Nixon advisor Herbert Stein . . . Looking toward his 1972 reelection campaign, Nixon was not going to let that happen again . . .
>
> So the central economic issue became how to manage the inflation-unemployment trade-offs in a way that was not politically self-destructive; in other words, how to bring down inflation without slowing the economy and raising unemployment. One approach increasingly seemed to provide the answer—an income policy whereby the government intervened to set and control wages . . . [The] Democratic Congress provided the tools by passing legislation that delegated authority to the president to impose a mandatory policy.

Not surprisingly, some within the Republican Party saw Nixon's wage and price controls as an unforgivable betrayal. Twenty years later, conservative *Wall Street Journal* editor Robert Bartley was still smarting: "I am willing to forgive [the Nixon Administration] Watergate, but I am not willing to forgive them floating the dollar and instituting wage and price controls . . ." (in the video "America's Political Parties: The Republican Party 1960-1992").

Somewhat more surprising was the significant amount of *support* that this "leftist" policy received from within Republican circles, including but not limited to the Nixon Administration itself. And then again, to the members of the APSA Committee who had decades before criticized the lack of clear and coherent ideological differences between the two major parties, this turn of events might have been seen as a source of chagrin but hardly of surprise.

of manufacturing, communications, transportation, and/or utilities. In reality, governments in democracies have often owned such means of production as car or weapons manufacturers (e.g., British Leyland historically and France's GIAT/Nexter today), television and radio stations (e.g., Norway's NRK and Britain's BBC), airlines (e.g., Air Canada and British Airways historically, and Air India today) and railroads (e.g., Amtrak today and Conrail historically in the United States), and large power producers (e.g., New Zealand's Mighty River Power, France's Électricité de France, and America's Tennessee Valley Authority). Even when not advocating government *ownership*, left-oriented parties are prone to favor substantial *regulation* of private sector companies on the grounds of assuring competitive fairness, health and safety of workers and consumers, and quality of production. Parties of the right tend to oppose government ownership, favoring private ownership of most if not all means of production, and are even wary of government regulation of the private sector.

Placing the Parties Along the Left-Right Continuum

Having identified four major issues on which parties might be differentiated for our purpose, positioning the parties along the left-right continuum, the next step is to determine what the parties' official positions actually are on each of those issues. While that obviously requires carefully reading each party's platform/manifesto, it also requires a systematic way of assigning a particular "position" (i.e., "number") along a numerical left-right scale to the words that we have read there.

Our own approach starts with development of a "coding scheme" for each of the four issues. The coding scheme describes what would be found in platforms that would justify positioning parties at various locations along the scale from "extreme left" to "extreme right," and assigns numbers to those locations. "Coders" who are responsible for reading the platforms and assigning the "codes" (i.e., numbers) first read all statements in a platform that pertain to a particular issue, compare what they have read there to the descriptions in the coding scheme, chose the best "match," and assign the appropriate code/number.

Box 2.4 contains the coding scheme for the issue "Control of the Means of Production." Numerical scores for this variable—as for each of the four issue variables—range from –5 for the "extreme left" position to +5 for "extreme right," with 0 assigned to the ideological "center." Coders were told to assign to each party's platform the most appropriate code from the 11 whole numbers ranging from –5 to +5.

Box 2.5 contains summaries of what the coders found on this issue in the Democratic and Republican platforms of 1952. Having read and summarized the Democrats' platform content, and then comparing that content to the descriptions in the coding scheme, the coder determined

Box 2.4 Coding Scheme for "Control of the Means of Production"

–5 (PRO-strong)
Strongly favors government ownership; advocates governmental owner-ship of all basic industries; advocates government ownership of means of production generally.

–3 (PRO-moderate)
Favors government ownership, but with some limitation; advocates government ownership of some basic industries but not all; may advocate acquiring some industry not currently under government ownership, while it could oppose acquiring something else.

–1 (PRO-weak)
Advocates very limited government ownership, with the limitations clearly stated; would oppose moves to have government take over most basic industries, for instance, but tends to base its preferences in this regard on practicality rather than principle.

0 (NEUTRAL)
Has contradictory positions that seemingly offset one another, and/or is truly "centrist" on the issue.

+1 (ANTI-weak)
May grudgingly accept very limited government ownership, but tends to oppose extension to additional industries, and certainly opposes the idea of governmental ownership of all basic industries; may advocate returning some government-owned industry to private ownership, while stopping short of advocating that all government industries should be returned.

+3 (ANTI-moderate)
Opposes government ownership generally, on principle; may advocate returning one or more government-owned industries to private ownership as a short-term measure, while probably holding return of all remaining state-owned industries as a long-term goal; would oppose government assuming ownership of any industry now in private hands.

+5 (ANTI-strong)
Strongly opposes government ownership as intolerable; would advocate immediate return of any government-owned industry to private ownership.

Source: Janda (1980: 55–56)

that the numerical code of "+1" (for Anti-weak, or "Weak Right") was the appropriate numerical code. In a context where the government owned few means of production and engaged in only a moderate level of regulation, the Democratic Party generally accepted that status quo though advocating some minor reduction of regulation in particular areas and as changing conditions might allow. Hardly a ringing endorsement of a strong governmental hand in controlling the means of production, yet hardly a strong repudiation of the status quo! "Weak Right" seemed appropriate, given the advocacy of some reduction, and the "+1" was assigned as the Democratic Party's position on this variable for 1952.

Having followed that same process for each of the parties' platforms, for all four issues, our coders assigned the sets of codes indicated in Table 2.1. As illustrated there, we use the "average" (i.e., arithmetic mean) of a party's four separate issue codes as its platform's overall "left-right position." On a left-right scale ranging from −5 to +5, the Democrats' average score of −1.50 places them slightly to the left of the ideological center point, while the Republicans' score of +1.25 places them slightly to the right of center. While some might interpret this as having two "middle-of-the-road" parties, the ideological distance that separates them (the 2.75 units between −1.50 and +1.25) could still be substantial enough for voters to meaningfully differentiate between the two parties.[1]

The APSA Committee clearly thought the American parties were too close together, ideologically, to fulfill the needs of their "responsible parties" model. The Report pulled no punches: "alternatives between the parties are defined so badly that it is often difficult to determine what the election has decided, even in broadest terms" (pp. 29–30). But their assessment of the American parties was partly a result of comparison to Britain's major parties, which they observed to be much more easily differentiated by their electorate. In spite of Britain's sharing with the United States the two-party system and plurality elections, the proponents of the Report argued, the more "responsible" British parties still provided their voters with clear (or at least clearer) programmatic differences. The American parties, on the other hand, seldom provided meaningful differences in their platforms, which the APSA Committee apparently saw as just hodgepodges of issue stands rather than as coherent programs.

Our own systematic comparison of the two pairs of parties, though, reveals an interesting inconsistency between the reality and the APSA Committee's assumptions. Table 2.1 includes the relevant information for this U.S.–U.K. comparison.[2] While the British parties include one—Labour—that was clearly not a "middle-of-the-road" party (with an average position score of −3.25), they also include another—the Conservative Party—which, despite its name, was actually slightly to the left of center (−0.75). The amount of "distance" between these U.K. parties was 2.50, which is actually slightly less than the distance of 2.75 between the American parties. While we would not want to go too far in arguing that

Box 2.5 Codes and Supporting Documentation for Democrats and Republicans, 1952

Democratic Platform of 1952

Code: +1

The Democratic platform includes the following statements:

> Independent business is the best offset to monopoly practices. The government role is to insure that independent business receives equally fair treatment with its competitors;
> ... [W]e urge the enactment of such laws as will provide favorable incentives to the establishment and survival of independent businesses ...
> We pledge a continuing increase in the services of the United States Postal Service.

While this platform praises the private sector and certainly does not call for expansion of governmental ownership, neither does it explicitly call for returning governmentally owned business to the private sector (and in fact acknowledges the importance of the Postal Service).

Republican Platform of 1952

Code: +3

The Republican platform includes the following statements:

> We condemn the President's seizure of plants and industries to force the settlement of labor disputes by claims of inherent Constitutional powers.
> ... We vigorously oppose the efforts of this national Administration, in California and elsewhere, to undermine state control over water use, to acquire paramount water rights without just compensation, and to establish all-powerful federal socialistic valley authorities.
> ... We favor restoration of the traditional Republican public land policy, which provided opportunity for ownership by citizens to promote the highest land use.
> ... We pledge a more efficient and frequent mail delivery service.

It appears that the party wants the return of some industries (but apparently not the Postal Service) to the private sector, and certainly opposes on principle any growth in ownership by government.

Table 2.1 Ideological Positions and Consistency, United States (1952) and United Kingdom (1955)

	Dems 52	*Reps* 52	*Labour* 55	*Cons* 55
Means of Production	+1	+2	−3	+2
Public Welfare	−3	+1	−5	−3
Redistribution	−1	+1	−1	−1
Econ Decision-Making	−3	+1	−4	−1
Ave. left-right score	−1.50	+1.25	−3.25	− .75
Left-right "distance"	2.75		2.50	
INconsistency	1.50	.38	1.25	1.38
Average INcons.	.94		1.31	

this is evidence that the American parties were significantly *further apart* than the British parties, it can certainly be taken as evidence that the British parties were not significantly further apart than their American counterparts, as the APSA committee had assumed.

On a different dimension of the ideological content of the parties' platforms/manifestos, the Committee called for more "coordinated and coherent programs" (p. 31). Rather than consistent ideological approaches, what they allegedly saw instead in the United States were hodgepodges of inconsistent issue positions. Our data again support a different conclusion than that assumed by the APSA Committee. Their Report would have led us to expect much more consistency within the British manifestos, but our data actually reveal a slight edge in favor of the American parties. With "consistency" (or more appropriately, "inconsistency") measured as the "average deviation from the mean" for the four individual issue position scores, *smaller* average deviations indicate *greater* consistency. On that basis, as is evident in Table 3.1, it may be true that both British parties had slightly more consistent (i.e., less INconsistent) programs than the Democratic Party, but it was the Republican party that had the most consistent program of all. Indeed, on average, the American parties' platforms were slightly *more* consistent than the British parties' electoral manifestos. Again, the difference may not be substantial, but what difference does exist is not in the direction the APSA Committee would have led us to expect.

So, whether considering ideological consistency or ideological distance, our conclusion is that the APSA Committee's assumption of a clear edge for the British parties cannot be supported with our data. Even if the slight advantages found for the American parties are due to nothing more than small errors of coding, it is at least unlikely that the British parties held the large edge that the APSA Committee seemed to assume (see Box 2.6).

Box 2.6 Where Do the American Parties Fall on Cultural Supports?

Beyond the obviously "economic" variables that we have included in our composite measure of parties' left-right positions, there are narrower issues that—while not obviously "economic"—still reflect the parties' orientations toward the role of government in matters that could presumably be left to the private sector. One such matter is "culture." As a political issue, one question with relevance to finances is whether the government should provide economic supports for the arts. Our coders have again examined the manifestos of numerous parties with an eye toward coding—still on a scale from –5 to +5—the positions of the parties on government supports for culture.

At the extreme left end of the scale could be found positions such as that taken by the Danish Social Democratic Party in 1980: "Art in all its forms of expression and the consumer's choice of cultural activity should be guaranteed independent of commercial interests" (for a code of –5). On the extreme right are positions such as that taken by the Danish Progress Party in 1989: "public regulation and public supports for cultural activities should cease to exist" (for a +5). While both the U.S. Democratic and Republican parties (from 1952 through 2012) have most commonly taken rather centrist positions (often earning codes of –1) on public cultural supports, the Democrats have sometimes veered further to the left and the Republicans further to the right, though never reaching the ultimate extremes on the scale. For example, the Democrats in 1972 were coded as –3, with the platform including the statement "We should expand support to the arts and humanities by direct grants through the National Foundation for the Arts and Humanities, whose policy should be to stimulate the widest variety of artistic and scholarly expression." In 1992, the Republicans veered to the right and earned a code of +4 with a platform including the statement ". . .no artist has an inherent right to claim taxpayer support for his or her private vision of art if that vision mocks the moral and spiritual basis on which our society is founded. We believe a free market in art—with neither suppression nor favoritism by government—is the best way to foster the cultural revival our country needs."

How Could the APSA Committee Have Gotten This So Wrong?

Indeed, the APSA Committee's conclusion that the American parties were not "responsible parties" was not developed in a vacuum; instead, it was in large part the result of direct comparison to the parties of Great Britain.

Had the committee members not been so convinced that the British parties they observed were providing voters with clear, coherent, programmatic choices, they may not have seen the American parties as so deficient in those areas. The direct U.S.-U.K. comparison was in many respects the starting point for the Responsible Parties Report and the assumptions on which it was based.

So, then, how could those assumptions have been so faulty, at least with regard to the comparisons on ideological distance and programmatic consistency? Where the APSA Committee assumed the American parties provided far less ideological choice and consistency than the British parties, we have systematically compared across the two countries and have reached far different conclusions. Far from providing significantly *greater* ideological distance and consistency, our data suggest that the British parties may actually have been providing slightly less of both. At the very least, there was very little difference between the United Kingdom and the United States in the amount and coherence of choice being provided their major parties.

The British party system did differ from the American system, though, in two ways, both of which may help explain how the Committee's members may have reached their assumptions. First, whereas the two American parties hovered around the ideological center, leading to their image as two "middle-of-the-road" parties, the British system included one centrist party (the Conservatives, who were actually slightly left of center) and one that was arguably "leftist" (the Labour Party). This could be one reason why the British parties, in spite of actually providing slightly less distance between them than the American parties, might have *appeared* to provide a clearer choice.

Another likely factor is the greater cohesion of the British parties in their legislature. In Figure 2.1, we have attempted a graphic comparison to illustrate the point (and, undoubtedly, exaggerate it to some degree). In the 1950s, the Democratic party in Congress still included many southern conservatives who often voted against the majority of their party who were liberal northerners, thus potentially contributing to some confusion as to what the "party" stood for. Likewise, in the Republican party were many relatively liberal representatives from New England states, who potentially contributed to a confusing image for that party as well. At the same time, the two British parties were highly disciplined and cohesive, almost always resulting in a solid bloc of Labour members voting against a solid bloc of Conservatives. When British voters—and the APSA Committee as well—observed what was happening in parliament, they saw something resembling two distinct blocs. American voters—and the APSA Committee—saw two overlapping clouds in Congress. The greatest inconsistency in the American case may, then, have been found not in the planks of a platform nor even in the positions taken by the party over time, but rather in the behavior of the party's legislators. It seems reasonable to conjecture that

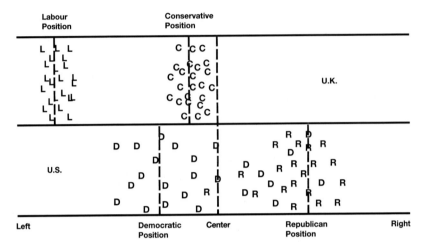

Figure 2.1 Hypothetical Images Provided by Legislators' Behavior

Source: Harmel and Janda (1982: 38)

given two party systems with all else equal, the one with the greater party cohesion will appear to provide more significant choices and in fact will provide its voters with greater *clarity* regarding the differences that actually do exist.

Why Did Both the U.S. and U.K. Systems Provide Relatively Little "Choice?"

While the U.S. parties may have indeed been at least as far apart as the British parties at the time of the APSA Committee's writing, the truth is that neither of those two party systems provided all that much "choice," as compared to the party systems of other democracies. Figure 2.2 is based on data produced in a similar way for 95 parties that existed at that time in 28 democracies around the world, including the four main parties of the United States and United Kingdom. It is readily obvious that these two systems' "ideological distances" are significantly shorter than is true of the average for the other countries. But something else is also quite apparent: it tends to be the countries with proportional representation (PR) electoral systems (i.e., those that tend to reward smaller parties with legislative seats more so than do the plurality systems of the United States and the United Kingdom), and that consequently have more parties, that produce the greater amounts of ideological choice. Parties that are small and more "ideologically extreme," whether on the left or right or both, can still be significant players in the politics of countries with PR such as the Netherlands, Luxembourg, and Sweden, and thus can add significantly to the range of choice provided to their voters.

To some extent, then, the nature of the electoral system may place structural limits on the range of choice that the country's parties can provide. In countries with plurality (i.e., "first-past-the-post") elections and single-member legislative districts, which tend to reward only "big" parties with legislative seats, two-party systems tend to result. And for both of those two parties to remain successful, neither can veer too far from that

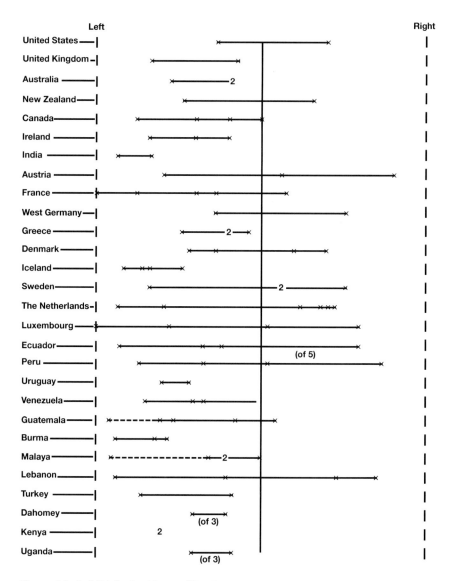

Figure 2.2 Left/Right Positions of Parties
Source: Harmel and Janda (1982: 29)

country's "ideological center." And hence, the range of choice is likely to be rather limited.

But even though the electoral system may set limits, it would be wrong to think that those limits are cast in stone, that they can never be altered or expanded. And that is because it is not just the electoral system that affects the shape of the party system; there are other important, variable factors as well. And this is certainly well illustrated in the more recent experience of the U.S. party system.

Expansion of the "Ideological Distance" in the U.S.

Though the significant features of the American electoral system at the national level have not been changed in any substantial way for many decades, most long-term political observers would agree that the Democrats and Republicans are certainly further apart today, ideologically speaking, than was the case in the 1950s. Adding our own coding of the two parties' left-right positions in their 2012 platforms, Table 2.2 makes clear the extent to which the distance between them has increased relative to 1952, with most of the change resulting from the dramatic shift rightward of the Republican Party.[3]

Though change of electoral system could not possibly explain this expansion of ideological distance in the U.S. (since electoral system change had not occurred), another factor that technically resided outside of the party system itself can go far in doing so. What at least began—in 2009— as a political movement *external* to the Republican Party, the Tea Party (which is not technically a *party* at all)[4] very quickly had a profound effect on politics *within* the GOP. Especially after a number of primary election victories by Tea Party-endorsed candidates in 2010, the Grand Old Party increasingly became (or certainly was perceived to have become) the host party for this right-wing political movement. And the 2012 Republican platform stands as clear testimony to that fact, particularly as contrasted to the program of just four years earlier.

Table 2.2 U.S. Parties' Left-Right Positions, 1952 vs. 2012

	Dems 52	Reps 52	Dems 12	Reps 12
Means of Production	+1	+2	−1	+4
Public Welfare	−3	+1	−4	+2
Redistribution	−1	+1	−1	+2
Econ Decision-Making	−3	+1	−2	+3
Ave. left-right score	−1.50	+1.25	−2.00	+2.75
Left-right "distance"	2.75		4.75	
INconsistency	1.50	.38	1.00	.75
Average INcons.	.94		.88	

As recently as 2008—prior to full-blown development of the Tea Party movement—the Republicans' platform called for an approach to regulation based "on sound science to achieve goals that are technically feasible," which would "protect against job killing intrusions into small businesses," while the 2012 platform went further to support "a sunset requirement to force reconsideration of out-of-date regulations" and to "endorse pending legislation to require congressional approval for all new major and costly regulations." The 2008 platform advocated that "federal agricultural aid should go to those who need it most as part of a sensible economic safety-net for farmers" and for "creation of Farm Savings Accounts to help growers manage risks brought on by turbulence in global markets and nature itself," while the 2012 platform admonished that "Just as all other federal programs must contribute to the deficit reduction necessary to put our country back on a sound fiscal footing, so must farm programs contribute to balancing the budget" and added that "programs like the Direct Payment program should end in favor of those, like crop insurance, that help manage risk and are counter-cyclical in nature." And regarding environmental policy, the 2008 platform acknowledged the environmental impact of increased "carbon in the atmosphere" and that "common sense dictates that the United States should take measured and reasonable steps today to reduce any impact on the environment," specifically arguing that "any [such] policies should be global in nature;" in 2012, though, the platform called for "a site- and situation-specific approach ... instead of a national rule" and a requirement of "congressional approval before any rule projected to cost in excess of $100 million to American consumers can go into effect." In each instance, it is not just the tone that had changed, but the substance as well, with the 2012 platform going further than the pre-Tea Party version in adding a sunset requirement and extensive congressional approval for regulation, ending certain agricultural subsidy programs, and limiting the scope of environmental policy.

In spite of these changes, the Republican Party could hardly be characterized as an "extreme right-wing party," even in the context of an influential Tea Party. And yet, it is clear that the party did move significantly rightward between 2008 and 2012, thus expanding its "ideological distance" from the Democrats, and pushing that range of choice toward the limits of what the current election system could reasonably be expected to allow. The APSA Committee called for clearer differences between the two parties as one condition for meeting the needs of party responsibility, and—though certainly not as a direct response to the Committee's call—its members would presumably be pleased to find the greater distance that exists between the Democrats and Republicans today.

Box 2.7 Where Do the American Parties Fall on HEALTHCARE?

One of the narrower issues on which parties normally demonstrate their broader left-right orientation is healthcare, and specifically what the government's role should be with regard to healthcare. Once again, our coders examined parties' platforms and assigned scores from –5 to +5.

The Danish Social Democrats in 1977 and the British Labour Party in 1987 give us good examples of parties advocating complete (or at least nearly complete) government ownership of the healthcare sector. The Social Democrats summarized their position (earning a –5) in two clear sentences: "Health care is to be provided by society. All employees, including doctors and dentists, are to be employed by the public sector." And Labour's position (also earning a –5) was just as clear: "Privatization means a health service run for profit rather than in the patients' interests. Labour will end privatization in the NHS [National Health Service], relieve the pressure on NHS facilities by beginning to phase out pay beds, and remove public subsidies to private health. Labour will establish the NHS in its rightful place as a high quality service . . . free at the time of use to all who need attention."

Indeed, in those two countries, where government-run healthcare is well established, even parties located further to the right have traditionally taken positions on healthcare that are clearly left of center. The British Conservatives have often taken positions deserving codes of –3 and so has the Danish Conservative Party, with the latter even reaching codes of –4. Another Danish party that had at times claimed the mantel of the country's only truly right-wing party, the Progress Party, received codes of –2 and –3 on government provision of healthcare.

In the United States, the Democratic Party had normally taken positions slightly to the left of center until 2008 and 2012, when its commitment to "Obamacare" justified codes of –3. On the other side, the Republican Party had normally taken positions at or just to the right of center until 2008 and 2012, when the party's reaction to Obamacare justified codes of +3. In 2008, the Democrats' platform included the statement that "Families and individuals should have the option of keeping the [insurance] coverage they have, or choosing from a wide array of health insurance plans, including many private health insurance options and a public plan. Coverage should be made affordable for all Americans with subsidies provided through tax credits and other means." In the same year, the Republicans' platform included the statement that "Republicans support the private practice of medicine and oppose socialized medicine in the form of a government-run universal health care system . . . We will not replace the current system with the staggering inefficiency, maddening irrationality, and uncontrollable costs of a government monopoly."

Projects and Exercises

Project 2.1: Coding "State Control of Means of Production"

In this project, you will get an opportunity to do a bit of "coding" yourself. We have chosen to have you do this for one of the key components of what we have called the left-right or "economic" dimension of politics: the degree to which the party advocates or opposes government control over the means of producing goods and services. We begin with some discussion of this issue and some examples of how our own coders have applied codes to some representative platforms.

State Control of Means of Production

This variable deals with the extent to which a party wants the government to control the means by which products and services are produced in the country. While government regulation of private sector production is included under this concept, the even more obvious examples of government involvement in control over means of production is for the government itself (i.e., the government on behalf of "the public" in general) to actually own and operate the means of producing goods and services. Examples might include the government owning major airlines and railroads (i.e., means of transportation), farms, or major industries. In the United States, examples of government ownership include the postal service and Amtrak. On this variable, the Democrats have normally hovered around the center (receiving codes of –1, 0, and +1 in the period 1952 through 2012), while the Republican Party has ranged from slightly to very right wing (receiving codes from +1 through +4, more often at the upper level). The Democrats' platform of 1964 and the Republicans' 1988 platform are representative (see Box 2.8).

For the U.K. parties, we would like you to get a bit of experience doing some "coding." On the basis of the information provided in each of the summaries below, and using the coding scheme provided in Box 2.4, what numerical codes would you give to the Labour Party for 1974 and the Conservative Party for 1992? Also, add a sentence or two to the summary, explaining why you think your code is appropriate given the information provided.

U.K. Labour 1974

Your Code: _____

"In addition to our plans for taking into common ownership the land required for development, we shall substantially extend public enterprise by taking over mineral rights. We shall also take ports, ship-building, ship-repairing and marine engineering, and the aircraft industries into public ownership and control. We shall not confine the extension of the public sector to loss-making and subsidised industries. We shall set up a National Enterprise Board to administer

Box 2.8 Codes and Supporting Documentation for Democrats and Republicans, 1964

1964 Democrats

+0

While regulation is not mentioned directly, the platform does include statements pertaining to protection of consumers. "Where protection is essential, we will enact legislation to protect the safety of consumers and to provide them with essential information. We will continue to insist that our drugs and medicines are safe and effective, that our food and cosmetics are free from harm, that merchandise is labeled and packaged honestly, and that the true cost of credit is disclosed." With regard to ownership, the platform mentions (and apparently passively accepts) federal direct involvement in power production and federal development of an oceanography exploration fleet. On the other hand, the party clearly intends continued support of the private sector. "We will stimulate as well as protect small business, the seed bed of free enterprise and a major source of employment in our economy. . .It is the national purpose, and our commitment to increase the freedom and effectiveness of the essential private forces and processes in the economy. Our present prosperity was brought about by the enterprise of American business, the skill of the American work force, and by wise public policies." In this platform, the party neither states opposition to currently held public enterprises nor does it advocate for increased public ownership, and statements regarding regulation are limited to commitments to protect consumers. A "truly neutral" code of 0 seems appropriate here.

1988 Republicans

+4

In this platform, the party clearly states its intentions to move in the direction of privatization in at least many of the areas in which the government has been an owner, and to keep government out of production in other areas. "We resolve to defederalize, denationalize, and decentralize government monopolies that poorly serve the public and waste the taxpayers' dollars . . . We advocate privatizing those government assets that would be more productive and better maintained in private ownership. . .We will not initiate production of goods and delivery of services by the federal government if they can be procured from the private sector." As for regulation of the private sector, "we must redouble our efforts to cut regulation, keep taxes low, and promote capital formation to sustain the advance of science and technology." The platform also applauds President Reagan and Vice President Bush for "relieving Americans from oppressive and unnecessary regulations and controls." Together, these statements justify a code of +4.

publicly-owned share-holdings: to extend public ownership into profitable manufacturing industry by acquisitions, partly or wholly, of individual firms. . ." The manifesto also states that "wherever we give direct aid to a company out of public funds we shall in return reserve the right to take a share of the ownership of the company." This manifesto does not mention regulation of the private sector, perhaps because of the emphasis placed on government ownership. **Why is your code appropriate?**

_____

_____

_____

_____

U.K. Conservative 1992

Your Code: _____

"Competition and private ownership are the most powerful engines of economic efficiency, innovation and choice. They lead to the creation of world-class companies. We have returned to private enterprise two-thirds of the companies once owned by the state: 46 businesses employing about 900,000 people. . .We will continue our privatisation programme. British Coal will be returned to the private sector. So will local authority bus companies. We will encourage local authorities to sell their airports. We will end British Rail's monopoly. We will sell certain rail services and franchise others . . . The Ports Act 1991 has paved the way for the privatisation of the Trust Ports by competitive tender. Tees and Hartlepool, Tilbury, Medway, Forth and Clyde have already been privatised. We are privatising Northern Ireland Electricity and will privatise the Northern Ireland water and sewage services. We will look for ways of bringing private sector skills into the management of Northern Ireland Railways." With regard to regulation of the private sector, the manifesto says, "We are concerned that at every level of government some regulations may have been adopted in answer to legitimate concerns, but without proper regard to their overall impact on business and individuals. A proper balance needs to be struck between essential protection for the public, and overzealous and intrusive controls aimed at the elimination of all conceivable risk." It goes on to say that "Existing regulations which are outmoded and burdensome must be simplified or removed." **Why is your code appropriate?**

_____

_____

_____

_____

Exercise 2.1: Measuring Ideological Consistency

One measure of "consistency" (or rather "inconsistency") of a party's positions on multiple left-right issues is what is called the "average deviation from the mean." In other words, it is a measure of the average amount of distance of the party's individual issue scores from the party's own average issue score. The larger that "average deviation from the mean," the more the party is "jumping around" ideologically as it moves from one left-right issue to another; lower scores will be achieved when the party is staying ideologically consistent as it moves from issue to issue. In Table 2.1, we have reported the INconsistency scores for the two major American parties (1952) and two major British parties (1955).

To see how these scores were actually computed, complete the exercise below. Begin by determining the number of units (i.e., the "distance") between each party's mean ("average") score and each of its individual issue positions. Then add up those four "deviations from the mean" and *divide* that number by the number of issues (i.e., 4).

For the Democrats in 1952, the individual scores for each of the four left-right issues are +1, –3, –1, and –3, as shown in Table 2.1. The average of those four scores is –1.50.

The number of units between

> +1 and –1.50 is 2.50
> –3 and –1.50 is 1.50
> –1 and –1.50 is .50
> –3 and –1.50 is 1.50

The sum of those "deviations from the mean" is 2.50 + 1.50 + .50 + 1.50 = 6.00.

And 6.00 / 4 = 1.50, which is the average deviation from the mean, or the Democratic Party's INconsistency score.

Now do the same for the Republicans in 1952 and Labour and the Conservatives in 1955, using the data provided in Table 2.1. Be sure to show all of your work.

Exercise 2.2: Difference Between Ideological Position and Ideological Consistency

It is widely assumed that the truly "ideological" (or "programmatic") parties will both have a relatively extreme ideological position and be ideologically consistent, while "pragmatic" parties will have more centrist positions overall and "shop around" for issue positions that please the voters whose support they are seeking, thus being less ideologically consistent. While this is generally the case, there are certainly exceptions to the general rule.

Below is a diagram presenting a visual picture of a party that was truly ideologically extreme (on the left) and also consistent across its positions, the Social Democratic Party of Denmark (using their 1961 manifesto).

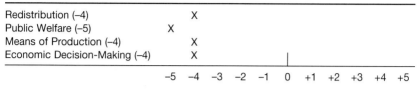

Redistribution (–4)					X						
Public Welfare (–5)		X									
Means of Production (–4)			X								
Economic Decision-Making (–4)			X								

-5 -4 -3 -2 -1 0 +1 +2 +3 +4 +5

Denmark: Social Democratic Party (*extreme left* and *consistent*)

Complete the diagrams for the U.S. Democrats and Republicans and for the U.K. Conservatives. Indicate each party's positions on the four separate issues with X's. Fill in the two blanks with the appropriate designations for overall ideological position and consistency/inconsistency. To what extent do these "visual images" match up with what is presented in Table 2.1?

Redistribution (-1)
Public Welfare (-3)
Means of Production (+1)
Economic Decision-Making (–3)

-5 -4 -3 -2 -1 0 +1 +2 +3 +4 +5

United States: Democratic Party 1952 (_____ and _____)

Redistribution (+1)
Public Welfare (+1)
Means of Production (+2)
Economic Decision-Making (+1)

-5 -4 -3 -2 -1 0 +1 +2 +3 +4 +5

United States: Republican Party 1952 (_____ and _____)

Redistribution (-1)
Public Welfare (-3)
Means of Production (+2)
Economic Decision-Making (–1)

-5 -4 -3 -2 -1 0 +1 +2 +3 +4 +5

United Kingdom: Conservative Party 1955 (_____ and _____)

Project 2.2: Interpreting the U.S./U.K. Differences

Writing in 1955, political scientist David Butler of Oxford University assessed the differences between the Conservative and Labour parties of Great Britain and between the Republicans and Democrats in the United States, and concluded:

> The choice may seem more *confused* in the United States, but it is more *far-reaching*. The parties in Britain may be *distinct* from each other, but they are not very *different* from each other.
>
> (Butler 1955: 52, emphasis added)

Regardless of what, specifically, Butler himself meant by those words, to what degree are they consistent with (a) the APSA Committee's assumptions that underlie their Report and (b) what we have found in our own analyses of the respective parties' platforms?

Project 2.3: Survey on Attitudes Toward "Choice" Provided by Parties

An underlying assumption of the APSA Committee seemed to be that the American parties were not providing a clear enough choice for the American voters. Presumably, the parties were too close together in their policy positions to give the voters as clear a choice as they might desire. But how much choice is "enough?" In 1964, political scientist Jack Dennis surveyed 702 Wisconsin adults and asked them a number of questions about their attitudes toward parties and the party system in the United States. Among those questions were two that bear directly on the question of "How much choice does the American public want the parties to provide?"

On the question of whether the respondents agreed or disagreed with the statement "The parties do more to confuse issues than to provide a clear choice on them," Dennis found that 54 percent agreed with the statement, and 21 percent disagreed (with the remainder saying either "neither agree nor disagree" or "don't know"). But in answer to a second statement that presumably would offer a solution to what 54 percent saw as a problem, "Things would be better if the parties took opposite stands on issues more than they do now," only 31 percent agreed and 43 percent disagreed.

Unfortunately, there has been no subsequent report of later surveys that asked the same questions. So while we know what some Americans felt about "party choice" in the 1960s, we don't know what Americans might feel today.

Though it would not be possible for you alone to survey a large enough group of American voters to produce a scientifically valid study, it would nonetheless be interesting to know how your family and friends feel about the amount of "choice" offered by the Democrats and Republicans today.

With your instructor's help, design and implement a questionnaire that includes at least the two questions mentioned above. And if you like, you could add these additional questions, which were also included in Dennis's survey:

Do you agree or disagree with the following statement? "The conflicts and controversies between the parties hurt our country more than they help it."

Circle one: Agree / Disagree / Neither Agree nor Disagree / Don't Know

Do you agree or disagree with the following statement? "The political parties more often than not create conflicts where none really exists."

Circle one: Agree / Disagree / Neither Agree nor Disagree / Don't Know

If you would like to read more about what Dennis found in his study, and see even more of the questions that he asked, read Dennis (1964).

Notes

1   These data are slightly different from those used for Harmel and Janda (1982), reflecting the different sources of basic information used for the 1982 project. While those data were coded on the basis of what coders learned about the parties' positions from reading multiple sources including secondary literature, the information on which our data are based is limited to just the parties' official platforms/manifestos.

2   We should note that our data do not match perfectly to the time period when the APSA Committee was observing and writing. In order to use platforms that contained adequate information for coding all four issue positions, while staying very close to 1950, we used the 1952 platforms for the American parties and the 1955 manifestos for the British parties. Though these platforms/manifestos are not ones that the APSA Committee could have read prior to writing their Report, they are still of essentially the same time period and follow essentially the same format as earlier platforms/manifestos, while providing sufficient information for coding all of the necessary issue positions.

3   As noted by Thomas Mann (2014), political science studies of behavior in Congress have shown that "it would be a mistake to equate the two parties' roles in contemporary political polarization. The Tea Party has moved the GOP even further from the political center. . ." (see McCarty et al. 2008). And beyond Congress, Mann (2014) argues, "changing Republican Party positions on taxes, Keynesian economics, immigration, climate change and the environment, healthcare, science policy, and a host of cultural policies are consistent with the pattern."

4   Some have argued that since the Tea Party is not really a party, the words should not be capitalized. Nate Silver, for instance, in the fivethirtyeight.com blog (May 22, 2014) argues: "Perhaps it's time to discourage the use of 'tea party.' Or, at the very least, not to capitalize it as *The New York Times* and some other media organizations do. 'Tea Party' looks better aesthetically than 'tea party,' but triggers associations with a proper noun and risks misinforming the reader by implying that the tea party has a much more formal organizational infrastructure than it really does." While we certainly do not want to suggest greater organizational infrastructure than the group has, we have nonetheless made the decision to capitalize here for the "aesthetic" reasons Silver implies.

3 Organization
How Well Organized Are the Parties?

Aside from the adoption of the direct primary, organizational forms have not been overhauled for nearly a century. The result is that the parties are now probably the most archaic institutions in the United States.

(Responsible Parties Report 1950: 25)

Introduction

Leon Epstein, a parties' scholar and contemporary of the APSA Committee of 1950, wrote in 2002 that back in those earlier days, he—along with other students of parties—tended to greatly value "a British party's mass-membership organization" and its supposed influence "in committing elected legislators to a set of policies."

> In that light, the Report's proposal to develop mass-membership parties looked like a means to help achieve programmatic party cohesion.
>
> (p. 203)

Indeed, whether put in terms of "mass party organization" or simply "more and better organization," it is very clear that the Committee thought the American parties were under-organized, so much so that improved organization would be necessary in order to accomplish its other, loftier ambitions for the parties.

While better organization could not by itself result in responsible parties, it would be necessary in order to achieve greater nationalization of power, greater cohesion within the legislative parties, and ultimately, greater clarity for the voters. As put in the Report itself:

> Broad governmental programs need to be built on a foundation of political commitments as written into the programs of adequately organized parties.
>
> (p. 31)

Box 3.1 What Is Meant by "Mass Membership Party?"

In the United States, it is commonplace to hear people say they are "members" of the Democratic or Republican parties, and yet most of those do little more for their party than regularly (or even not so regularly) vote in its primary elections or vote for its candidates in general elections. In many European democracies, being a "member" of a party means much more than that. At the least, members may be required to pay dues to the party organization. Beyond that, some parties require their members to make a commitment to support the party's policy positions, and some require members to regularly participate in party activities. The Austrian People's Party, for instance, has required payment of membership fees, active support of the party's programmatic goals, and willingness to work in the party's organization and to participate in membership recruitment (Katz and Mair 1992: 52). The Irish Fianna Fail has required new members to sign a card declaring acceptance of the party's constitution and all members must actively participate in local party activities and particularly election activities; in addition, a member must not be "guilty of conduct unbecoming a member of the organization" or face expulsion from the party (Katz and Mair 1992: 406).

This European approach is consistent with the notion that members not only belong to the party, but the party also "belongs" to the members. In this sense, a party's members are distinguished from its voters, who "support" it but don't "own" it. Members are "part of" the party; voters support it from the outside.

In the United States, where the parties don't have members in that sense, the more appropriate distinction is between a party's "activists" and those who merely vote for its candidates. The activists do more than simply vote, but they stop short of being "card-carrying, dues-paying" members of the party in the European sense.

It is probably little wonder that party reformers generally focus at least some of their attention on how—and how well—parties are organized. Like all organizations, parties involve recurring interactions among individuals based on a division of labor and differentiation of roles; the nature and extent of a party's organizational structure is bound to have consequences for its activities and performance. Maurice Duverger, one of the foremost students of party organization, has said that organization:

> constitutes the general setting for the activity of members, the selection of leaders, and decides their powers. It often explains the strength and efficiency of certain parties, the weakness and inefficiency of others.
>
> (Duverger 1961: 4)

It is the organizational aspect of political parties that gives them substance and identity apart from their prominent candidates and leaders of the moment. As James Q. Wilson (1973: 7) has put it: "Organization provides continuity and predictability to social processes that would otherwise be episodic and uncertain."

In a word, then, organization *matters*, or at least that's what the APSA Committee assumed. Valuing strong organization, they were essentially appalled by what they saw in the two major parties. In spite of "marked changes [that] have occurred in the structure and processes of American society during the twentieth century, . . . formal party organization in its main features is still substantially what it was before the Civil War" (p. 25).

While party organization at the state and local levels might have been adequate, at least in states where the two parties were competitive, neither of the parties had given much attention to "the question of adequate party organization at the national level" (p. 25). Among the deficiencies, "the parties have not yet established research staffs adequately equipped to provide party leaders with technical data and findings grounded in scientific analysis" (p. 31). Coordination among the levels of organization was so lacking that "the national and state party organizations are largely independent of one another, each operating within its own sphere, without appreciable common approach to problems of party policy and strategy" (p. 26). The national conventions were, in their words, "unwieldy, unrepresentative, and less than responsible" (p. 28). And though widely thought of as "membership organizations," these were virtually parties *without* members, at least in the European sense of dues-paying, card-carrying members. "No understandings or rules or criteria exist with respect to membership in a party" (p. 27).

To rectify the situation, the Report (Appendix A) urged reducing the size of the national conventions but holding longer and more frequent meetings—once every two years rather than every presidential election year. It called for development of a regional level of organization, for more frequent local party meetings, for greater investment in campaign organizations for congressional candidates, and for enlargement and strengthening of staff (especially for research) at permanent national headquarters. It also proposed the creation of a "party council" for each party consisting of 50 members, who would meet at least quarterly to make a preliminary draft of the party platform, interpret the platform in relation to current problems, make recommendations to appropriate party organs regarding congressional candidates, bring to the attention of the national convention or committee conspicuous departures of state or local party organizations from national party decisions, discuss and perhaps screen presidential candidates, and just generally help to better coordinate the activities and communications among the existing party organs. Finally, the Report also envisioned development of true party "membership" in the European sense, with specified expectations and requirements for those who would presume to be called and treated as party members.

In this chapter, we begin by testing the APSA Committee's assumption that the American parties were much less well organized than their British counterparts, then put the American parties' levels of organization within a broader context to assess whether those levels were at least adequate to support the responsible party model, and then consider whether they have become more or less well organized since the time of the Committee's work.

How to "Measure" Party Organization

In political science literature on party organization, it is generally accepted that "how well" a party is organized equates to how complex and active its organization is. For instance, how many separate "organs" exist for carrying on party activities at the national level, how small are the smallest units of party organization at the local level and how widely spread are those units across the country, how adequate are a party's record-keeping and research capabilities, and how frequently do the party's membership organizations actually meet? In other words, how elaborate is the party's organization? (We should note here that "how well" a party is organized does not equate with the question of "where the power lies" within the organization. That will be the subject of Chapter 4 on decentralization of power.)

In order to compare parties across different countries in their levels of organizational capacity, our own approach started with developing coding schemes for six different dimensions, including each of those mentioned above (Janda 1980). Several of these relate directly to organizational components of concern to the APSA Committee.

Two of the six are indicators of how well organized a party is at the national level:

- "**structural articulation**," scored from 0 to 11, with higher scores assigned when there are numerous national organs that have clearly specified functions to carry out; and
- "**records and research**," scored from 0 to 16, with higher scores indicating greater capacity for carrying out such basic organizational activities as research, publication, and record-keeping.

Three of the indicators tap into the degree of lower-level party organization and activity:

- "**intensiveness of organization**," referring to the relative size of the party's smallest organizational units and scored from 1 (where the national level is the only level of party organization) to 6 (where the lowest level involves 100 members or less, as in the case of communist party cells);

- "**frequency of local meetings**," tapping the level of activity of local organizational units and scored from 0 to 6, with higher scores assigned when local meetings are frequent; and
- "**extensiveness of organization**," referring to how widespread are the smallest units of organization and with scores ranging from 0 to 6; higher scores apply when the country is thoroughly covered, lower scores when the smallest units are concentrated in just part of the country.

Because some parties are advantaged by having outside organizations assist in doing what would otherwise be seen as "party business"—for instance, labor unions mobilizing support for Labour parties or churches doing so for Christian parties—we also measure:

- "**pervasiveness of organization**," scored from 0 to 18, with higher scores assigned when a party is supported by large "ancillary organizations" across many sectors of society.

While it might seem reasonable to assign codes for these variables on the basis of information contained in a party's own official rules, it turns out that parties' official documents would often be inadequate for the task. While formal party statutes tell the "official story" of what the statute-writers wanted for the party's organization, they often do not convey the complete or true story. While rules may mandate that local parties should meet monthly, for instance, the reality may be quite different. Because we are concerned with the reality of party organization, our coders were instructed to base their codes on information from whatever reliable sources they could find, including secondary literature on the parties.

Organizational Capacity of the American Parties, 1950

The first two columns of Table 3.1 are our codes for the American parties for the six indicators of organizational capacity discussed above. At the time the APSA Committee was producing its Report, both American parties had four staple organizations at the national level (national convention, national committee, and House and Senate campaign committees) plus a number of auxiliary organs (e.g., women's organizations and college-level organizations). At the "most local" level, both parties were organized mainly on the basis of precincts, which typically encompassed 1,000 or fewer voters. The Democrats' precinct organizations were found virtually throughout the country, exceptions being in parts of New England and the Midwest; the Republicans scored a bit lower on this variable since they lacked active local organization in much of the South. For both parties, local organizations tended to meet only during campaigns. Both parties maintained a publishing program and research divisions, though those activities were more active within the Republican Party. Both maintained some mailing lists for fundraising purposes, but these were hardly complete and fell far short of membership lists maintained by parties elsewhere. The Democrats received outside organizational support from labor unions at both the state and national levels, while the Republicans' allied organizations were limited to their women's and youth groups.

With both parties receiving relatively high grades on four of the six indicators, a first impression might be that the American parties were not so badly organized after all. But the APSA Committee was not viewing the American parties in a vacuum; it was more concerned with their organizational capacity *relative to* that of other parties, and especially the British parties. We turn to those comparisons now.

Placing the Parties Comparatively on Party Organization

Table 3.1 contains the results of the coding for all six indicators of party organization, for the four major parties of Great Britain as well as the United States, as they looked in the early 1950s. Though *on average* the British parties held an advantage over the average for the American parties on pervasiveness of organization and a slight advantage on extensiveness, the American parties *on average* held a slight advantage on intensiveness and a very slight advantage on structural articulation. On research and record-keeping, the British parties outdistanced the Democrats but not the Republicans. It was only on frequency of local party meetings that *both* U.K. parties clearly bettered both of their American counterparts. Bottom line: U.K. parties win by decision, but hardly the knockout punch that the APSA Committee might have led us to anticipate!

Broader Comparison

To make these and other comparisons more straightforward, though, it would clearly be advantageous to have an "overall" measure of organization, much as we did for "ideological position" in Chapter 2. This time,

Table 3.1 Codes for Indicators of Organizational Complexity, Early 1950s

	United States		United Kingdom	
	Dem	Rep	Con	Lab
Structural Articulation (0–11)	10	10	9	10
Intensiveness (1–6)	5	5	4	4
Extensiveness (0–6)	5	4	6	5
Frequency of Local Meetings (0–6)	2	2	6	6
Records and Research (0–16)	8	12	12	12
Pervasiveness (0–18)	7	3	6	10

though, simply taking the average across the six indicators is not an option. This is because the ranges of scores are so different across the six variables (e.g., 1–6 for intensiveness of organization but 0–18 for pervasiveness). A 6 on intensiveness clearly does not have the same meaning as a 6 on pervasiveness. So before averaging, we must first somehow "standardize" the scores (i.e., force them all onto the same scale).

The procedure for doing this is called "standardized scoring" (or z-scoring). Without going into what, exactly, is involved in the process, suffice it to say that in a perfect world the end result would always be a scale ranging from roughly –2.5 to +2.5 with an average score of 0. This is not a perfect world, but we can still say that the scales produced for all six indicators would *approximate* that range and mean. At the very least, the procedure results in scales that are similar enough across the indicators to make averaging meaningful.

Having averaged across the standardized scores for the six indicators of organization, Table 3.2 presents comparable scores for "overall organization" for the U.S. and U.K. parties as they looked in 1957–1962.[1] Our conclusion from "eyeballing" the data of Table 3.1 is confirmed in Table 3.2: the U.K. parties were indeed better organized than the American parties, just as the APSA Committee had assumed.

Comparing more broadly—across a sample of 95 competitive parties in 28 democracies in the 1957–1962 period—we find that the actual range of scores for overall organization is from 1.15 at the top (the Social Democratic Party of what was then West Germany) to –2.70 (the Liberal Party of Greece), with an average of –.13. So, as is evident from Figure 3.1, while the U.K. parties were better organized than the U.S. parties, the British parties were not the most organized parties in the world. And in fact, they were not all that much better organized than the American parties. And the American parties were, after all, better organized than the "average" for competitive parties around the world.

So while the APSA Committee may have been correct in its assumption that the U.S. parties lagged behind their U.K. counterparts on degree of organization, it would not appear from our data that the difference was so great as to account for the alleged difference between responsible and irresponsible parties. The American parties—with multiple functionally specific organs and some research and record-keeping capacity at the national level plus widely spread, relatively small units of organization at

Table 3.2 Comparison of "Overall Organization," 1957–1962 Period

U.S. Democrats	+.12
U.S. Republicans	–.02
U.K. Labour	+.62
U.K. Conservatives	+.50
All competitive parties (mean)	–.13

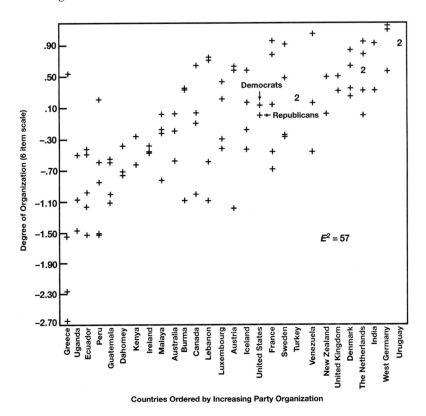

Figure 3.1 Degree of Party Organization, Averaged by Country
Source: Harmel and Janda (1982: 45)

local level—were certainly sufficiently well organized to provide the organizational requirements for even the "responsible" model of political parties.

Why Both the U.S. and U.K. Parties were Relatively Well Organized

As with the two countries' comparative placements on ideological distance (Chapter 2), the U.K. and U.S. parties were actually more similar with regard to their levels of organization at the time of the writing of the Report than they were different. Both countries' parties were relatively well organized in the 1950s, and all four parties were above the average for all competitive parties at the time. Given what it would take to produce complex organizations, this should not be surprising.

Systematic cross-national comparison of the 95 parties in 28 democracies has shown that modernity, population size, breadth of the electoral franchise (i.e., right to vote), length of experience with democracy, nature

Box 3.2 Extreme Examples of Party Organization: SPD of Then West Germany; Liberal Party of Greece

The Social Democratic Party of then West Germany and the Liberal Party of Greece stand at opposite ends of the ranking of parties on "organizational complexity" in the 1950s, as depicted in Figure 3.1.

The Social Democratic Party represents what was and still is generally true of parties of the left; they tend to be very organizationally complex, often with very small units of party organization spread throughout their country. (The former Communist Party of the Soviet Union was one of the most organizationally complex of them all, with "cells" of 100 or fewer members being the smallest unit of organization.) The SPD was coded with maximum scores on structural articulation (with four national organs having clearly delineated functions), intensiveness (with "cellular" organizational units at the local level), extensiveness (with cellular units throughout the country), and maintaining records, and next-to-maximum scores on the other indicators of complexity.

The then centrist Liberal Party of Greece (which in 1961 merged into the Center Union Party) had just two identifiable organs at the national level and almost no organization below that level. In spite of this, the party was still able to win 42 (of 300) seats in the 1958 parliamentary election, getting 20 percent of the vote and ranking third in electoral performance.

of the electoral system, and degree of party competition were all important factors in explaining why some countries' parties were better organized than others (Harmel and Janda, 1982). This is probably because more modern societies provided more of the necessary conditions for developing complex organizations and longer experience with democracy provided more time to do so, larger populations and especially larger electorates increased the need for complex parties to organize the masses of voters and potential voters, there is less need for a high degree of organization under plurality elections (where campaigns can be run by candidates rather than parties) and in noncompetitive situations (where neither the dominant party nor the always-losing party(ies) see much benefit from organization).

The American parties—operating in a modern country with a relatively large population and broad franchise, long experience with democracy, and highly competitive two-party competition in much of the country (the exceptions being the South and rural New England)—should have been expected to have well-organized parties. Only the plurality electoral system should have pulled in the other direction. The environment in the United Kingdom was quite similar in many respects, including the plurality form of elections. And indeed, in both the United Kingdom and the United

Box 3.3 Parties and Their Environments

In a sense, the APSA Committee was recommending that the American parties "change themselves" into something they presumably were not: parties more like the British parties, in the responsible parties' mold. But are parties really free to shape themselves however they wish, and hence to make whatever organizational and profile changes they or others might like?

In fact, most serious students of parties agree that parties are profoundly affected by the contexts in which they reside. Longtime scholar of American parties William Keefe (1972: 1) famously said of those parties that "The parties are less what they make of themselves than what their environment makes of them." Of parties more generally, French political scientist Jean Blondel (1969: 125) has said, "in all cases, the influence of outside elements has played a part in the development or

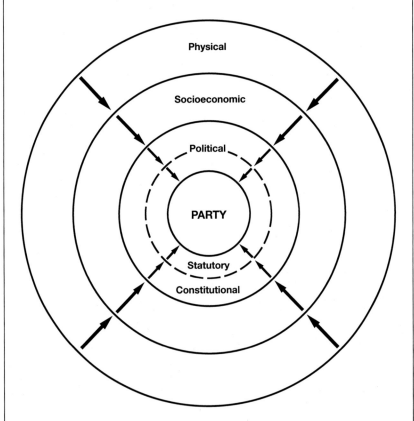

Figure 3.2 Parties and Levels of Their Environment

Source: Harmel and Janda (1982: 13)

modification of internal structures." Parties may, of course, choose to ignore the external pressures, but the desire to fit in sufficiently to be electorally successful could get them to think twice about doing so.

Where does the outside influence come from? In the pages of this book, we note that prior research has identified numerous factors that affect each of the dimensions of concern to us, and which effectively represent multiple levels of the "environment" within which parties live and operate. Of course, these factors actually vary a great deal across the world's countries and their party systems, thus helping to shape parties differently in different locations. First, there are physical factors, such as the size, shape, and climate of the country. There are socioeconomic factors, such as the racial and occupational composition of the society, the degree of urbanization, and the educational level of its citizens. Finally, there are political factors, such as the structure of the legislature, the type of electoral system, and the frequency of elections (see Figure 3.2).

Of course, parties can also affect their environments, just as their environments affect the parties. This is more true, however, of the political factors than of the socioeconomic factors, and of socioeconomic factors than of attributes of the physical environment, which are virtually immune to parties' attempts to change them. When we identify features of the environment that have helped to shape the American parties in ways that are relevant to the APSA Committee's preferences, you may want to consider the extent to which any or all of those external factors could be altered by the parties themselves, so as to make for a new environment more receptive to responsible parties.

States, the parties were already quite well organized by the 1950s, as their environments seemingly allowed and perhaps even demanded.

But just as changes in the parties' environment over time have resulted in changes on the ideological dimension (see Chapter 2), so too has the American environment changed in ways that could affect the parties' organizational arrangements and capacity.

Organizational Complexity and Capacity in the U.S. Parties Today

While it would be hard to argue that the U.S. environment has changed significantly since the 1950s on several of the factors known to affect organizational complexity, it has changed significantly on a few of them—in ways that could certainly impact party organization. While the population has grown to over 300 million, it was already a large enough country in 1950 (at around 150 million) to warrant complex organization. Though the Voting Rights Act of 1965 effectively expanded the franchise in parts of the South, the electorate was already extensive in the 1950s. Though some states have tinkered with their election laws, the basic structure of plurality elections with single-members districts for Congress and the Electoral College for the presidency are still intact. And while the country is 60 years older, it was already a well-established democracy at the time the APSA Committee was writing its Report (see Table 3.3).

On "modernity" and "competitiveness," though, there have been significant changes. American society has moved past "modern" to "postmodern" on the heels of the technological/computer revolution. It is hard to imagine now, but parties' lists of donors and activists were once recorded by hand (if at all), and maintained in rows of file drawers or cardboard "bank boxes." With the advent of computers that were affordable and accessible to office workers, parties had the option of significantly enhancing their record-keeping, and both American parties moved in that direction. Computers also affected the way in which research could be conducted, making it much easier not just to maintain, but also to analyze volumes of data on voters, donors, and public opinions. And in fact, both American parties have significantly expanded and improved their "records and research," as reflected in the substantial changes in their scores on this variable between the 1950s and 2010.

The parties' political environment has also changed significantly over the past several decades. Once noncompetitive, one-party areas of the country—the "Democratic South" and "Republican Rural New England" —both became much more competitive. In the South, at least, this occurred first in national politics and then in local politics as well (see Hershey 2013: 30). As a consequence, Republicans saw new advantage in developing local party organization in the South, and the Democrats presumably did likewise in New England.[2] For their parts, the once-dominant parties saw new benefit in enhancing their local organization as well.[3] The extent of these changes was not substantial enough to affect the score of the Democrats on "extensiveness of organization", and development or enhancement of Republican organization in substantial parts of the South

Table 3.3 Codes for Indicators of Organizational Complexity, 1950 vs. 2010

	Democrats		Republicans	
	1950	2010	1950	2010
Structural Articulation (0–11)	10	10	10	10
Intensiveness (1–6)	5	5	5	5
Extensiveness (0–6)	5	6	4	6
Frequency of Local Meetings (0–6)	2	2	2	2
Records and Research (0–16)	8	12	12	16
Pervasiveness (0–18)	7	7	3	3

Box 3.4 The Democratic Party Midterm Convention and Charter of 1974

Though the roots of the Democratic Party reach back into the late nineteenth century, it was not until well into the twentieth century that it developed a written constitution for itself. In fact, when delegates met at a midterm convention in Kansas City in 1974, the Democrats did what no major American party in history had done—wrote a constitution for the party itself. Parties' scholar William Crotty has summarized the importance of the meeting in these words: "Its intent was to revitalize and modernize structures that had evolved with little change since the late 1840s" (Crotty 1977: 252).

The 1974 Charter did call for some significant organizational changes. The Democratic National Committee was to be increased to 350 members, the Executive Committee was reconstituted by providing for half the delegates to be selected by regional caucuses of National Committee members, and new organs were to be established in the form of a Judicial Council, a National Finance Council, and a National Education and Training Council. While not all of these intentions were fully implemented, the act of formulating the Charter was itself a monument to new self-awareness of the party as a national organization.

In addition, the document has been seen as reflecting especially the interests of reformers bent on further democratizing the inner workings of the party. One article (Article 10), for instance, is labelled "Full Participation," and admonishes that "Discrimination in the conduct of Democratic Party affairs on the basis of sex, race, age (if of voting age), religion, economic status or ethnic origin is prohibited, to the end that the Democratic Party at all levels be an open party." And another (Article 6) provides for an additional set of national conventions (called "national party conferences") to be held between the presidential nominating conventions. But the calling of these "midterm conferences" is left to the national committee, which has not done so since 1982, due both to cost and to the perception that the midterm conventions of 1978 and 1982 had proven to be more divisive than unifying (e.g., see *Chicago Tribune* 1985).

The full text of the 1974 Democratic Charter is available online as an appendix to Harmel and Janda (1982).

---

justified an even larger coding change. While for parts of the South the period of close two-party competition has proven to be merely a stage of transition to Republican dominance (Hershey 2009: 29), the organizational legacy of the more competitive period remains.

So, the evidence suggests that the American parties were already quite well organized in the 1950s, largely because their physical, social, and political environments were conducive to well-organized parties. And since then, they have become somewhat better organized, particularly in the aspects of extensiveness (especially for the Republicans) and records and research (for both parties). While the APSA's Committee would presumably look with favor on such changes, it is highly unlikely that the parties changed in response to their Report. Instead, it is reasonable to attribute the greater organization to a couple of important environmental changes that occurred later: the technological/computer revolution and broader two-party competitiveness across the country.

Projects and Exercises

Project 3.1: Subnational Party Organization in the United States

At the national level of party organization in the United States, both parties have both "temporary" and "permanent" units of organization. The temporary units are the national conventions, which meet only once every four years, in presidential election years. The permanent units consist of the national committees, the national chairpersons, and the funding units of the parties.

The major parties also have organizational units at the state and local levels in each of the states, and both temporary and permanent units also exist at those levels. Search in relevant books and online to find information about party organization in your own state, and answer the following questions:

1. What temporary and permanent organizational units exist at the state level?
2. What temporary and permanent organizational units exist at the county level?
3. What temporary and permanent organizational units exist at a level (or levels) below the county level?
4. If there are any temporary or permanent organizational units between the state and county levels, what are they?
5. How are the leaders of the party organizations at each of those levels chosen (e.g., appointed, elected, chosen by some other means)?

Project 3.2: Local Party Websites

One mark of party organization at the local level today is the extent to which a local party maintains a website for communicating to its members or to the public in general. Beyond just possessing such a site, it is also informative to know what content the party includes at the site, and the quality of its presentation. The contents and appearance of the website might be useful indicators of the extent to which the local party is active and organized.

Go to the websites of the Democratic and Republican parties for the county in which your academic institution is located, and check off which of the following features you see:

- _____ A link for donating money to the party (2)
- _____ Information about upcoming elections (e.g., election dates, offices up for election) (1)
- _____ Location of local polling places (1)
- _____ Information on how to register to vote (1)
- _____ Contact information for the party (2)
- _____ List of county/precinct chairs (2)
- _____ County party bylaws (1)
- _____ List of opportunities for volunteering for the party (2)
- _____ The national, state, and/or county party platform (1)
- _____ News stories (1)

Now add up the number of points (found in the parentheses after each item) for the items you have checked above. Divide that total by the maximum number of points available (14) (e.g., 10 points earned/14 points possible = 71.4). The resulting number is the website's "content score." _____

Then check which of the following apply to the site:

Pictures/logos

- _____ No pictures and/or logos (0)
- _____ A few pictures and/or logos (1)
- _____ Multiple pictures and/or logos (2)

Currency

- _____ Contents appear to be dated (0)
- _____ Contents appear to be up to date (2)

Navigation tools

- _____ Relatively difficult to navigate (0)
- _____ Relatively easy to navigate (1)

Independent website?

- _____ Independent website (1)
- _____ Website hosted by another entity (e.g., the state party) (0)
- _____ Page of a social media website (e.g., Facebook) (0)

Now add up the number of points for the four items you have just checked above. Divide that total by the maximum number of points available (6). The resulting number is the website's "quality score." _____

And now add up the total number of points for all of the items above (under both "content" and "quality"). Divide that number by the maximum number of points available (20). The resulting number is the website's "overall score."

Compare the various scores across the parties that you have included in this project. What do you conclude concerning the relative organizational capacity of these parties from the comparison of their websites?

Exercise 3.1: Do Party Reforms Matter? Representation of Women in National Conventions

In 1972, each Democratic state party organization was required by the McGovern-Fraser Commission rules to provide representation of women in its national convention delegation roughly equal to their percentage of the state's population. Republican state parties, at roughly the same time, were also encouraged (but not required) to increase representation of women and minorities in their convention delegations. Since 1980, the Democrats' state parties have been

Table 3.4 Percentage of Female Delegates

Year	Total Delegates Republican[1]	Number of Female Delegates Republican*	Percentage of Female Delegates at Republican Convention	Total Delegates Democrat[2]	Number of Female Delegates Democrat*	Percentage of Female Delegates at Democratic Convention
1932	1,154	87		1,154	134	
1936	1,003	61		1,100	165	
1940	1,000	78		1,100	125	
1944	1,056	100		1,176	139	
1948	1,094	112		1,234	155	
1952	1,206	127		1,230	155	
1956	1,323	208		1,372	158	
1960	1,331	201		1,521	154	
1964	1,308	233		2,316	331	
1968	1,333	223		2,622	349	
1972	1,348	402		3,106	1,239	
1976	2,259	712		3,008	1,013	
1980	1,994	716		3,331	1,659	
1984	2,235	1,073		3,933	1,947	
1988	2,277	829		4,161	2,031	
1992	2,210	928		4,288	2,131	
1996	1,990	653		4,289	2,140	
2000	2,066	702		4,339	2,091	
2004	2,509	1,104		4,353	2,168	
2008	2,380	762		4,419	2,165	

* Estimated using data from Freeman (2008: 140, Table 10.1).
1. Data from CQ Press (2010: 29, Figure 3.1).
2. Data from CQ Press (2010: 29, Figure 3.1).

required to provide roughly equal representation for men and women in their delegations (i.e., without regard to their percentages of the population). Using the data presented in Table 3.4, first produce percentages of total convention participants who were women, by party. Then discuss whether the "rules" and even the "encouragement" appear to have had the intended consequences for representation and participation of women in party decision-making, at least as applies to national conventions.

Notes

1 The codes used for producing the standardized placements of the parties cross-nationally for Table 3.2 are slightly different than those reported in Table 3.1. The data in Table 3.1 were produced in the 1990s by coders at Texas A&M University for the Party Change Project (PCP), whose purpose was to generate *annual* codes for over-time comparisons within the United States and three other countries, including the United Kingdom. But in order to produce meaningful standardized scores, to place the U.S. and U.K. parties in a much broader comparative context, and to produce useful analyses of how parties' "environments" affect them ideologically, organizationally, and behaviorally, we need data for many more parties in a broader range of democracies than just the four that were included in the Party Change Project.

Fortunately, very similar coding procedures were used a few decades earlier by a different set of coders for the International Comparative Political Parties (ICPP) project at Northwestern University (Janda 1980). The coders of the ICPP produced a broader data set for the purpose of comparing parties across many countries (including 28 democracies) at the same time, with each piece of data referring to the way a party looked during a "time slice" of six years, 1957–1962. Though the variables and coding schemes were the same for the two projects, the resulting data codes are different in a few instances. While this indicates that the coding procedures are not perfectly "reliable," the similar procedures and the significant amount of identical coding certainly justify the use of ICPP data in the broadly cross-national research reported here (most of which was originally produced for Harmel and Janda, 1982).

It is highly unlikely that either the relative placements of the American parties or the other Harmel/Janda results reported here would have been significantly affected by using the ICPP codes for 1957–1962 rather than the PCP's codes for 1950. For the record, the respective codes from the ICPP are (with Democrats' score listed first, Republicans' second): Structural Articulation (10, 10), Intensiveness (5, 5), Extensiveness (6, 5), Frequency of Local Meetings (2, 2), Records and Research (9, 12), and Pervasiveness (7, 3). It is those codes that were standardized and averaged for the "overall organization" scores reported in Table 3.2.

2 As noted in Reichley (1992: 396): "Prior to the 1960s, local Republican organizations were virtually unknown in much of the South, and Democratic organizations were similarly scarce in part of New England and the Midwest." While empirical evidence supports the conclusion that party organization improved in the South as competition increased between the parties, the evidence for rural New England is less consistent and so less conclusive (e.g., see Cotter et al. 1984).

3   As Lockard (1959: 45) noted with regard specifically to Vermont, "If Vermont continues to become more industrialized and more heavily urban in population, the Democrats may begin really to threaten on election day. The pressure will be on the Republican party to cease being the loosely disorganized instrument that it is now." As for the South, Cotter et al. (1984: 31) note concerning the early 1960s that "the traditionally dominant Democratic party had never found it necessary to organize and Republican organizational efforts were only just beginning." But by the 1980s when they were writing, "southern Republican parties [had] changed most dramatically, from a condition of very little organizational strength to one of above average strength (despite some decline during the 1970s)."

4 Decentralization

Where Does the Power Lie?

> Decentralization of power is by all odds the most important single characteristic of the American major party; more than anything else, this trait distinguishes it from all others. Indeed, once this truth is understood, nearly everything else about American parties is greatly illuminated.
>
> (E.E. Schattschneider 1942: 129)

Introduction

Writing three decades later than Schattschneider, Keefe (1972: 25) noted that "there is no lively debate among political scientists concerning the dominant characteristic of American political parties. It is, pure and simple, their decentralization." Indeed, the APSA Committee members wrote in 1950 that "the familiar description of the parties as loose confederations of state and local machines [with little or no national control] has too long remained reasonably accurate" (p. 25).

While the authors of the Report argued for more organization (Chapter 3) and ideological clarity (Chapter 2) in the American party system, they were *emphatic* about the need for strengthening the American national party organizations relative to their state and local counterparts: local party organizations should show "loyalty" to the whole organization, and national organizations should "deal with" disloyal state organizations (pp. 47–48). How, the authors wondered, could the American parties put forth coherent programs, require their elected officials to support those programs, and ultimately provide the voters with a vision of unified, well-organized parties, if the national parties lacked the power to control either their state and local namesakes or even their own national business?

Though the Committee's view that the American parties *were in fact* decentralized was widely shared in the political science community, there was less agreement with the Report's assertion that they *could be* less so. Given the environment within which the parties were operating, the critics argued, could the American parties centralize, even if they wanted to, and still remain viable political entities? Or put another way: were parties'

Box 4.1 Hierarchy vs. Stratarchy

It has often been noted that a distinguishing characteristic of American parties is that while many parties elsewhere have organizations that are clearly "hierarchical," the American parties are better described as "stratarchical." In a hierarchical arrangement, decisions would tend to be made at the top of the organization, and then flow downward for implementation. But in a stratarchy, different levels of organization exist (e.g., at the national, state, and local levels in the United States) but there can be no assumption of decisions flowing from the top downward.

The late political scientist Samuel Eldersveld, who is credited with attaching the term to the American parties in a 1964 publication, has put it this way:

> By a *stratarchy* is meant an organization with layers, or strata, of control rather than one of centralized leadership from the top down. At each stratum, or echelon, of the organization there are specialized organs to perform functions at that level. Each stratum of organization is relatively autonomous in its own sphere, although it does maintain links above and below. There is, thus, the proliferation of power and decision making and a recognition that lower levels are not subordinate to the commands or sanctions of higher strata.
>
> (Eldersveld 1982: 99)

---

structures so constrained by forces external to the parties that internal reform efforts might be irrelevant at best or at worst disastrous?

The APSA Committee clearly felt that more party centralization could be achieved as an internal party affair, without changing the constitutional system within which the parties operated. The Report did recognize the decentralization of the American government (as formalized in its federal structure) and the presidential system with its separation of powers as hindrances to party centralization, but not insurmountable hindrances. So instead of suggesting constitutional change, the Committee proposed a number of structural changes within the parties themselves. For instance, as summarized by Turner (1951: 149, with page references removed), the Report prescribed "that the parties deal with rebellious state delegations by excluding them from national conventions and from national committee posts, by using national party funds to defeat local officers, and by appointment of temporary state officers," all by way of strengthening the hand of the national parties vis-à-vis their state affiliates. As Kirkpatrick (1971: 968) puts it in his later review of the Report and related literature, the Committee's proposals were based on the assumption that

"Naturally, some restructuring of national party organizations would be required to provide strong, representative, policy-oriented leadership. It would be essential to reform the existing relations between state and local parties, on the one hand, and national parties on the other." The charge to the parties was clear: change yourselves!

But considerable doubt was raised about parties' abilities to change *themselves* by such parties' scholars as Turner (1951), Epstein (1967), and Keefe (1972). Keefe's assertion that "the parties are less what they make of themselves than what their environment makes of them" has echoed through much subsequent literature on the American parties. If such factors as large country size, separation of powers, and the federal system of government had led to the decentralization of the American parties, then what likelihood of success would there be for a party's unilateral attempts to alter its structure?

How to Compare Party Decentralization of Power

When describing the American parties, some observers (including academic writers) seem to equate the concepts of organization and decentralization, but these two important aspects of party structure can and should be carefully distinguished. That is, they are *not* the same thing! Where organization refers to the number and functional specificity of organizational units within the party, decentralization (and its opposite, centralization) refers to the distribution of power among the levels of organization. A party may be well organized while still being decentralized, and a highly centralized party may (at least hypothetically)[1] be lacking in complex organization. As we have seen in Chapter 3, the American parties were—already at the time of the APSA Committee's work—quite well organized, but it is still possible that they were also as decentralized as the Committee assumed.

As we are using the term here, "decentralization of power" refers to the distribution of control over decision-making among the levels of party organization—national, regional (where applicable), and local. In particular, the concept involves the extent to which the national level of party organization is free from control by the regional and the local levels in conducting what would normally be considered national party business and is capable of enforcing its decisions on the subnational organs.

In listing the areas of party decision-making that are most important to winning governmental office and conducting the party's other ongoing business, one would certainly include: (1) selection of candidates for the national legislature; (2) administration of party discipline; (3) allocation of funds; (4) selection of party leadership; (5) involvement in communications media; and (6) formulation of party policy. What level of the party, for instance, should decide who will represent the party as its candidates for the national legislature; should it be decided strictly at the constituency level or some other local level, or should there be involvement (perhaps including veto power) by some national body? Who should decide when, and how, to discipline party members (including especially those in public office) who fail to conform to expected behavior? Should this be done at the national level or at more local levels of party organization? At what level(s) should decisions be made about how the party's money should be spent? Should a party's national leader be selected solely by some unit of national organization (e.g., by a national executive committee) or should the process include a tier of organization closer to the party's members (perhaps even a vote of the members themselves)? Who should control content of the party's messages in the media: just the national party, or should flexibility be allowed for alternative messages at more local levels? And what level or levels should decide what the party "stands for," especially at election time?

Those six areas of party decision-making underlie our measurement of decentralization, with another indicator added to tap the more general, structural embodiment of decentralization. The seven measures used for rating parties on this concept are:

- "**selection of legislative candidates**," scored from 1 to 9, with low scores given to parties where selection is done by a national organ;
- "**administration of discipline**," scored from 0 to 4, with low scores given to parties where a national organ administers discipline over party members;
- "**allocation of funds**," scored from 0 to 6, with low scores given to parties where party funds are collected and allocated primarily by the national level;
- "**selection of national party leader**," scored from 0 to 8, with low scores given to parties with selection by a national party organ;
- "**involvement in communications media**," scored from 0 to 7, with low scores given to parties where the national (rather than regional or local) level of organization controls important party media;
- "**formulation of party policy**," scored from 0 to 7, with low scores given to parties where policies are formulated by a national organ; and
- "**nationalization of structure**," scored from 0 to 6, with low scores given to parties where there is a hierarchical structure with the national level in ultimate control.

Because we are focusing on the extent to which parties are *decentralized*, high scores on each of these variables indicate a high level of decentralization in the decision-making process while low scores indicate centralization (i.e., nationalization).

As was the case with our assignment of codes for the "organization" variables (Chapter 3), our coders were instructed to go beyond just the official story as presented in party rules and to consider information from a range of reliable sources, including secondary literature. Thus, our focus continues to be on the "real" story, whether that conforms to the official story or not (Janda 1980).

Decentralization of the American Parties, 1950

The first two columns of numbers in Table 4.1 are our codes for the American parties for the seven indicators of decentralization discussed above. On six of the variables—parliamentary (i.e., congressional) candidate selection, discipline, national leader selection, control of communications, policy formulation, and nationalization of structure—the Democrats and Republicans received the same scores. Both parties received the highest score for "parliamentary selection" since the national parties played no role in selection of their candidates for Congress, who instead were typically chosen by voters in primary elections "back home." Both parties also received the highest possible code on administration of discipline because neither party had effective means for disciplining members of Congress who bucked the party line. The only time when either party had a single, dominant "spokesperson" (i.e., a single national party leader) was during presidential campaigns, and presidential candidates of both parties were selected by national conventions, whose delegates were chosen at the state or congressional district levels. With regard to "control of communications," neither U.S. party published its own influential newspaper—as was sometimes done by parties in Europe—and there was virtually no control over statements made by state and local parties. When it came to shaping the parties' national election platforms, the central role was assigned to national conventions, made up of delegations from the states. And in both parties, national committees existed, but their membership was determined by state parties, and they were not considered to be more powerful than organizational units at the state and local levels.

Only on "allocation of funds" did the two parties receive different codes. Both national parties relied to some extent on collection of "quotas" from their state affiliates, but only the Republican party had a "finance committee" to coordinate fundraising at the national level. Since who is collecting the funds likely indicates who decides how the money will be spent, Republicans received a slightly less "decentralized" score than the Democrats for this variable.

With both American parties receiving scores in the "more decentralized" halves of the scales for a majority of these indicators, and receiving the maximum scores for two of them, just "eyeballing" the data might suggest that the parties were indeed quite decentralized. A more meaningful appraisal can only be made in comparison to other parties, however, and that comes next.

Box 4.2 Decentralization of Presidential Nominating Procedures

For the earliest presidential elections in the United States, the nominees of the major parties (once there were parties) were selected by the parties' congressional caucuses. These became increasingly unpopular as others within the parties complained of being shut out of the process; this resulted in some state parties nominating their own presidential candidates as well. Beginning in the 1830s, the "king caucus" was replaced by national conventions, with the intention of "opening up" the process. However, the selection of state parties' delegates to the national conventions was often done in "smoke-filled rooms" by state party officials, limiting the extent to which the process was indeed "open." While primary elections offered a means by which greater openness in delegate selection could be assured, primaries were used in only a minority of states until the mid 1970s. Since then, the number of states using primaries to select the parties' national convention delegates has mushroomed; in 2008, 67 percent of Democratic delegates were selected by primary in 39 states, while 82 percent of Republican delegates were selected in primaries in 42 states.

With each successive move toward greater "openness" in the presidential nominating process, there has been decline in the ability of the national party organization—and for that matter party organization generally—to control the outcome. Today, with primary voters arguably the most important decision-makers, the process is clearly one of the most decentralized imaginable.

Box 4.3 Party Control of Communications Media

How have changes in the vehicles used for mass communication—from newspapers to television to the Web—affected the ability of national parties to control the messages they wish to convey to the public?

During the first half of the twentieth century, national parties in many European democracies owned and directly operated newspapers, giving party officials complete control over the editorial and journalistic process. These newspapers were distributed nationwide, many available for purchase or for subscription by the entire populace. For example, in 1889, Austria's Socialist Party began publishing *Arbeiter Zeitung*, with the paper reaching a daily circulation of 100,000 by the 1920s. The French Communist Party has controlled publication of *L'Humanite* since formation of the party in 1920. The Social Democratic Party (SPD) of Germany began publishing *Vorwärts* (*Forward*) as a daily newspaper in 1891, and even continued publication—from Paris—when the paper was outlawed by Germany's Nazi regime in the 1930s. Norway's Labour Party began publishing *Vort Arbeide* in the 1880s, and eventually developed its own press system involving more than 30 newspapers and a publishing house.

The American national parties never achieved the publication prowess of many of their European counterparts; they instead attempted to reach their members and supporters with monthly newsletters produced from small publishing offices. While it has been reported that at the beginning of the twentieth century, roughly half of all daily newspapers in the United States were affiliated with one of the major parties, this did not mean that the parties owned the papers or that party officials had any input over their editorial content. It meant only that the newspapers presented their stories from a partisan point of view (Iyengar 2011).

During the second half of the century—with the growing popularity of television—party newspapers declined even in Europe, along with print newspapers in general. Many saw dramatic reductions in circulation. Some dailies became weeklies, and even monthlies, before ceasing publication altogether. The Austrian Socialists' *Arbeiter Zeitung* first became an independent paper in the late 1980s, and then folded completely a few years later. The SPD's *Vorwarts* continues today, but now as just a monthly newsletter.

Though television would provide an alternative medium for parties to reach their members and supporters, the parties would lose the control over content that newspaper ownership had provided. Even in the United States, where newspapers had often performed the role of editorial allies for one or both of the major parties, the television age—at least in the beginning before the advent of cable—would prove more difficult. Parties that could once count on friendly coverage from either overtly partisan newspapers or newspapers with covert partisan connections now had to deal with broadcast television with limited channels. The limitations to access meant that government regulators placed a much heavier burden on broadcast TV to show balanced, non-partisan coverage of political news. For example, both the BBC (British Broadcasting Corporation) and commercial broadcasters in the United Kingdom operated under strict impartiality rules put in place by their government. In addition, American broadcast TV stations (ABC, CBS, NBC) were required to follow the Fairness Doctrine, which required honest, equitable, and balanced coverage of politically important issues. Overall, parties lost a great amount of control over the major form of mass communications in the era of broadcast TV dominance.

However, the current media environment has given all parties in Internet-abundant states the ability to regain some degree of control over their communications. The advent of the Internet and expansion of TV into cable and satellite forms have given rise to a media environment with an unprecedented amount of consumer choice, and parties have used this change in environment to secure a tighter hold on their media messaging, with official websites, email-based newsletters, and social media accounts delivering the party's official statements for anyone to access, from political journalist to common citizen. Parties themselves now have a completely controlled media vehicle to present their official message, despite competition from other sources, such as "party-friendly" and not-so-friendly media outlets, state parties, or the social media of individual party representatives. Parties no longer have to go through a mass media middleman in newspapers, radio, or TV in order to present their views, once again granting some degree of control over their communications and a greater degree of control over the dominant forms of media than they had a scant 25 years ago.

Table 4.1 Codes for Indicators of Decentralization, Early 1950s

	United States		United Kingdom	
	Dem	Rep	Con	Lab
Parliamentary Selection (1–9)	9	9	5	5
Discipline (0–4)	4	4	0	0
Funds Allocation (0–6)	4	3	4	1
Leader Selection (0–8)	5	5	1	4
Communications (0–7)	4	4	0	0
Policy Formulation (0–7)	2	2	0	2
Nationalization (0–6)	3	3	1	2

Placing the U.S. and U.K. Parties Comparatively on Party Decentralization

Table 4.1 lists our codes for the seven indicators of decentralization for the major parties of both the United States and the United Kingdom, as they looked in 1950.[2] On five of the seven indicators, both American parties were coded as more decentralized than both of their British counterparts. For funds allocation, both American parties were more decentralized than the Labour Party, though the Conservative Party's score equaled that of the Democrats and slightly outdistanced that of the Republicans. On policy formulation, both U.S. parties were as centralized as the Labour Party, but still more decentralized than the Conservative Party. This casual comparison suggests that the decision-making power was indeed much more decentralized in the American parties than in the British.

Broader Comparison

To put both the U.S. and the U.K. parties in much broader perspective and produce "overall decentralization" scores, we have followed the standardization procedures already discussed and used in the chapter on party organization (Chapter 3). Our conclusion from the casual comparison of scores for the various indicators—and also, by the way, the APSA Committee's assumption in this regard—are confirmed in Figure 4.2.[3] The American parties were indeed more decentralized, and markedly so, than their British counterparts.

In the broader comparison—covering the 95 competitive parties in 28 democracies—both U.K. parties were on the "centralized" side of the mean score, while both U.S. parties were far from that mean on the "decentralized" side[4] (see Figures 4.1 and 4.2). In fact, the American parties were both among the most decentralized handful of competitive parties in our entire sample. The most decentralized parties of all were the Blancos and Colorados of Uruguay and the Republican Party of the United States, with the Democrats not far behind.

Their places among the most decentralized parties support the claims of Keefe, Schattschneider, and others that a distinguishing feature of the American parties has been their degree of decentralization. Sitting in marked contrast to their American counterparts, the British parties and their much more centralized structures further confirm the APSA Committee's assumption concerning their relative positions on decentralization of power. But while the Committee may have been correct in its observation that the British parties maintained a much higher degree of national control, there could still be cause for doubt in its preference for transporting that type of structure to America. After all, the United States and United Kingdom provided significantly different environments within which their parties might succeed or fail; perhaps the U.S. environment would reject highly centralized parties of the U.K. type!

Why the U.S. and U.K. Parties Were So Different on Structure of Power

Unlike for ideological distance (Chapter 2) and degree of organization (Chapter 3)—where the U.S. and U.K. parties were found to be quite similar, in contrast to the assumptions of the APSA Committee—on centralization/decentralization of power, the two countries' parties were indeed very different in the 1950s. The Committee observed that the British parties had centralized power, while the American parties were distinguished by their decentralization; and they were right on this score!

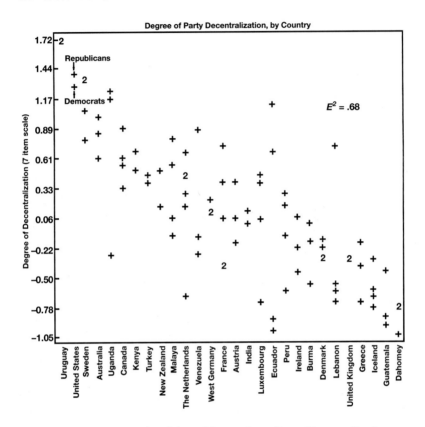

Figure 4.1 Countries Ordered from Most to Least Party Decentralization
Source: Harmel and Janda (1982: 61)

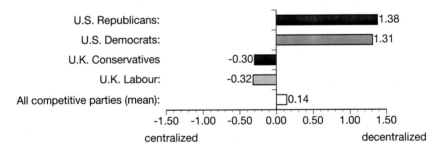

Figure 4.2 Comparison of "Overall Decentralization," 1957–1962 Period

Elsewhere (Harmel and Janda 1982), there has been systematic cross-national comparison of the 95 parties in 28 democracies, which has shown that the "environmental dimensions" of country size (i.e., geographical area), the "vertical" distribution of governmental power among levels of government, and presidentialism vs. parliamentarism were all important in explaining why some countries' parties tended to be more decentralized than others (recall Box 3.3). This is likely because large countries have greater need for institutions whose local branches are equipped to respond to localized needs and preferences, because winning important local offices within decentralized governmental arrangements may require customized electoral strategies and appeals, and because the need for centralized control of parliamentary campaigns where the party stands or falls together is lacking where separation of powers leaves congressional candidates to run (and for the most part, to fund) their own campaigns locally.

The British parties—whose environment included not only a relatively small country, but also unitary government (as opposed to federalism) and unified powers (i.e., parliamentarism) at the national level—could well afford parties with power concentrated at the highest level. But the American parties—seeking to win elections across an expansive country whose federalism created local offices worth winning and whose presidentialism left congressional candidates to appeal locally however they could—found themselves in an environment ill-suited to centralizing party power. Forcing all decisions from the top, and disciplining local campaigners for deviating from the national party line, would have been tantamount to inviting disaster. This was particularly true due to another important dimension of the political environment, itself related to the country's large size, and that was sectionalism. The party politics of the South were far different from those of other parts of the country, featuring a Democratic party whose candidates and platforms were far more conservative than those of northern Democrats. For the Democratic Party to continue its dominance in Congress and in controlling state governments, great latitude had to be allowed for the state parties in the South to forge their own—and very different—winning strategies.

Decentralization in the U.S. Parties Today

Since the time in the early 1950s when the APSA Committee wrote and published its Report, the geographical area of the United States has expanded, not shrunk, and little has been changed in the constitutional provisions regarding federalism and separation of powers. It would be naive, though, to think that the entire story of change in the physical and political environment of the American parties can be captured in numbers and laws. For while the area of the country has grown, the impact of "size" has to some extent been diminished by advances in communication and transportation technologies. Television and the Web have brought the problems and issues that were once considered just "local" or "regional" into dorm rooms and living rooms across the country, causing Americans to increasingly focus on the national level for solutions and accountability. And with greater public attention to the national level has come growing power there as well; just ask opponents of No Child Left Behind or the Affordable Care Act (aka Obamacare)!

Over the same period, nationalization of American politics also occurred, with reduction—or at least significant alteration—in the impacts of sectionalism for the two major parties. When sectional one-party dominance is a fact of politics, as was the case for the Southern (Democratic) and New England (Republican) sections of this country in the 1950s, national-level control would be extremely difficult, if not impossible. But over the subsequent decades, American politics has become more "nationalized" and less regionalized behaviorally, as evidenced in both electoral and congressional behavior. Where Southern voters had for so long elected conservative Democrats to Congress, they have for a few decades now been electing conservative Republicans instead. And where New England voters had previously elected liberal Republicans to represent them in Washington, most of those liberal Republicans have now been replaced by Democrats. As a consequence, the Democratic Party no longer has to be so concerned with granting sufficient local flexibility to win seats in the conservative South, and the Republicans needn't be concerned with allowing the latitude necessary to win liberal seats in New England. With greater "homogenization" of what it means to be Democrats or Republicans across the country, the parties have seemingly lost some of the need to be so decentralized.

But while the environment may have become incrementally more receptive to centralization of government power, and one might assume to nationalization of party power as well, the fact is that there have been few changes in that direction in the indicators we have coded. And the explanations for those changes have less to do with the country becoming more homogeneous or "smaller" than with other consequences of technological change. As shown in Table 4.2, changes in the direction of greater national control have occurred on just two of the seven indicators. The most dramatic changes, for both parties, have occurred in the collection and allocation of funds. When the APSA Committee was writing its Report, both national parties were heavily reliant on state parties for necessary funds, though the national level of the Republican Party wielded somewhat more control than its Democratic counterpart over allocation of funds. But by the late 1970s, the Republicans—under RNC Chair Bill Brock—had begun computer-assisted, direct mail fundraising. This effectively allowed the national party to bypass its state affiliates to raise its own money and hence to exercise total control over how that money would be spent. Beginning in the early 1980s, the Democratic Party followed suit, making it more dependent on multitudes of small contributors but far less dependent on its state parties. As an additional consequence, the state

Table 4.2 Codes for Indicators of Decentralization, 1950 vs. 2010

	Democrats			Republicans		
	1950	*2010*	*Change*	*1950*	*2010*	*Change*
Parliamentary Selection	9	9	0	9	9	0
Discipline	4	4	0	4	4	0
Funds Allocation	4	1	−3	3	1	−2
Leader Selection	5	7	+2	5	5	0
Communications	4	3	−1	4	3	−1
Policy Formulation	2	2	0	2	2	0
Nationalization	3	3	0	3	3	0

parties themselves became more "beneficiaries of" than "donors to" the growing national party coffers.

Smaller and yet significant changes have taken place with regard to control of party communications with supporters and the public generally. In 1950, neither national party had an institutionalized means of communication with its supporters. By the early 2000s, party organizations at all levels—including the national level—had entered the webosphere. While certainly not capable of single-handedly controlling all party communications, at least now the national parties had developed a means for directly transmitting their own messages (see www.democrats.org and www.gop.com).

When it comes to leadership selection, the Democrats buck the centralization trend and actually receive a more "decentralized" code for 2010 than they had received for 1950. At the time the APSA Committee wrote its Report, both parties' presidential nominees were selected at national conventions, where delegates had been chosen to represent state parties. That continued to be the case in the 2000s, though now the bulk of Democratic Convention delegates were being bound by national party rule to vote for particular presidential candidates, reflecting results of primary elections.[5] Given this important role of voters in primaries, the leader selection process (with the presidential candidate considered to be the party's leader and foremost spokesperson) is even more decentralized than when national conventions could act more independently when choosing the candidate. Paradoxically, it was a national party rule meant to limit state party control over delegates that ultimately resulted in an even more decentralized process.

So, while both parties may be slightly less decentralized overall than they were in 1950, they continue to be quite decentralized today, in spite of changes in their environment that might have allowed more centralization to occur. The limited changes in the direction of greater national party control—or at least involvement—were in part the result of the technological/computer revolution that made more feasible the mass mailings for fundraising purposes and made possible the development of party communication via the Web. Rather than being startled by the magnitude of these changes toward stronger national parties, though, the APSA Committee might well be dismayed by how little has actually changed in that direction. If the decentralized nature of party power stood in the way of more responsible parties in the 1950s—due to inability of the national level to control what was being done in the parties' names at lower levels of organization or even in the national legislature—then presumably that would still be a significant hindrance today.[6]

Exercises

Exercise 4.1: Organizational Capacity vs. Centralization of Power

The APSA Committee clearly felt that parties lacking in "organization" at the national level would be ill-equipped to "rule" the rest of their party and its representatives from that level. In other words, in order to have centralization of power, a party would need also to be well organized at the national level.

While the APSA Committee may have seen a distinction between organizational capacity and "power," some have treated the two concepts as effectively indistinguishable. We, on the other hand, have gone to great pains to treat them as separate dimensions of party structure, even devoting separate chapters to organizational complexity (Chapter 3) and centralization of power (Chapter 4).

In Appendix B, you will find data on both the structural articulation (*structartic*) and the nationalization of structure (*natofstruct*) for the competitive parties of 28 democracies as of the early 1950s. "Structural articulation" refers to the number of distinct organizational units at the national level of the party organization, and can be used as one way of measuring "how well organized" a party is at that level. "Nationalization of structure" captures the extent to which the relationship between the national level and more local levels of party organization conforms to a hierarchy, with orders flowing from the top (i.e., national) level of party organization downward to the lower levels. Nationalization of structure thus serves as one reasonable way of measuring the centralization of power within a party's structure.

To make it easier to analyze these data, we have "dichotomized" both variables. That is, we have reduced the original multipoint scales down to just two values for each variable. In the case of structural articulation, the value of "1" is applied to parties with fewer than four important organizational units at the national level, and a value of "2" signifies four or more such units. For nationalization of structure, the value of "1" is applied when the party lacks a clear hierarchy from top to bottom, and a value of "2" signifies a clear hierarchy from national to more local levels.

In the table below, enter the numbers of parties that qualify for each cell. For instance, in the upper left-hand cell, put the number of parties that are "decentralized" and have low organizational complexity. In the upper right-hand cell, put the number of parties that are "decentralized" and also have high organizational complexity, and so on. After these "frequencies" are placed in all four boxes, add up the numbers in the first column (upper and lower left-hand cells) and put the total on the blank line under that column. Do similarly for the right-hand column. Then divide each of the cell frequencies by its column frequency, and put that percentage in the cell, along with the cell frequency you have already placed there. Do this for all four cells. You now have what you need to do "cross-tabulation analysis." That's a fancy way of saying that you have what you need to see whether the data support the expectations: (1) that organizational complexity and centralization of power are indeed two separate concepts and not just one; and (2) that parties with low organizational complexity at the national level will lack the ability to control things from that level.

	Lo Org Complexity	*High Org Complexity*
Decentralized		
Centralized		

_____   _____

If "well organized" and "centralized" were the same thing, and "not well organized" and "decentralized" were the same thing, then there should be no parties in either the lower left-hand or the upper right-hand cells. Do you find any parties there? If so, you have some examples to support our own treatment of "organizational complexity" and "centralization of power" as two distinct concepts rather than just one overlapping concept. You may wish to identify and explore further the parties that fall into those two cells, which are high on organizational capacity but are still decentralized, or are low on organizational capacity but are still centralized.

It is the latter cases that actually should cause us to doubt the argument that without a high degree of organizational capacity, national parties cannot control what lower levels of party organization are doing in the party's name. The larger the percentage of parties with low organizational capacity that are nonetheless centralized, the greater the doubt that is cast on the latter argument. What percentage do you actually find in the lower left-hand cell? How much doubt does that create?

Exercise 4.2: Country Size and Party Decentralization

There are compelling reasons for expecting that countries with a large geographical footprint, such as the United States, will be more likely to have decentralized parties than is true of smaller countries. A few centrally-located leaders would find it more difficult to make all party decisions if the country is large than if it is smaller; a decentralized decision-making structure should make it easier to stay in touch with all parts of the population. In general, the larger the geographical area, the greater the need for decentralization in order to effectively "cover the field" of many diverse segments in the population, to administer the party's business more efficiently, and to allow some of the decisions—especially those of more concern locally—to be made locally. So, while this does mean that parties in small countries will need to be more centralized for opposite reasons, it also means that parties in small countries should not have as many reasons to be decentralized. It makes sense, then, to expect more parties in large countries to be decentralized than is true in small countries.

In Appendix B, you will find data on the geographical areas (*area*) in square kilometers for 28 democracies as of the 1950s, along with the scores for "Nationalization of Structure" for the parties in each of those countries during the same time period.

In the table below, enter the numbers of parties that qualify for each cell. For instance, in the upper left-hand cell, put the number of parties that are "decentralized" and are also found in small countries. In the upper right-hand cell, put the number of parties that are "decentralized" and are also found in large countries, and so on. After these "frequencies" are placed in all four boxes, add up the numbers in the first column (upper and lower left-hand cells) and put the total on the blank line under that column. Do similarly for the right-hand column. Then divide each of the cell frequencies by its column frequency, and put that percentage in the cell, along with the cell frequency you have already placed there. Do this for all four cells. You now have what you need to do "cross-tabulation analysis." In other words, you have what you need to see whether there is any support for our expectation that large countries are more likely than small countries to produce decentralized parties.

	Small Country	*Medium/Large Country*
Decentralized		
Centralized		

_____   _____

Compare the percentage in the upper left-hand cell to the percentage in the upper right-hand cell. Is the percentage in the right-hand cell substantially larger than the percentage in the left-hand cell? _____ If so, then our expectation is supported by the data.

Exercise 4.3: Polity Decentralization and Party Decentralization

According to political scientist David Truman (1955), "The basic political fact of federalism is that it creates self-sustaining centers of power, privilege and profit which may be sought and defended as desirable in themselves, as means of leverage upon elements in the political structure above and below and as bases from which individuals may move to places of greater influence and prestige in and out of government."

Indeed, federalism does create "centers of power" below the national level and spread across the country: local and regional centers worth competing for and winning. But it is not always the case that a party's national profile and campaign strategy will provide a winning formula in elections for all of those lower levels of offices. For that reason alone, the more local party organizations may demand — and may be granted — substantial flexibility. For several decades, for instance, the local Democratic organizations in the southern United States were allowed to run candidates on programs that often ran counter to the national party's program, all because it was deemed necessary to "decentralize" the party's power in order to win positions at all levels of government, in all parts of the country.

Does federalism — the decentralization of power in the structure of government — generally lead to *decentralization* of power in countries' parties? We have provided data in Appendix B that can be used to directly address that question. There, you will find data for whether the country is unitary or federal (*federalism*) and for "nationalization of structure" (*natofstruct*) for the parties of 28 democracies in the 1950s.

Of those 28 countries, six were federal systems with effectively decentralized power across the levels of government: the United States, Australia, Canada, India, West Germany, and Uganda.

In the table below, enter the number of parties that qualify for each cell. For instance, in the upper left-hand cell, put the number of parties that were "decentralized" and were also found in unitary countries (i.e., countries that did not have federalism). In the upper right-hand cell, put the number of parties that were "decentralized" and were also found in countries with federalim, and so on. After these "frequencies" are placed in all four boxes, add up the numbers in the first column (upper and lower left-hand cells) and put the total on the blank line under that column. Do similarly for the right-hand column. Then divide each of the cell frequencies by its column frequency, and put that percentage in the cell, along with the cell frequency you have already placed there. Do this for all four cells. You now have what you need to do "cross-tabulation analysis" to see whether there is any support for the expectation that countries with federalism are more likely than unitary countries to produce decentralized parties.

	Unitary	**Federal**
Decentralized		
Centralized		

Compare the percentage in the upper left-hand cell to the percentage in the upper right-hand cell. Is the percentage in the right-hand cell substantially larger than the percentage in the left-hand cell? _____ If so, then our expectation is supported by the data.

Notes

1   The APSA Committee might disagree, since the Committee seems to have assumed that nationalization of parties—which they clearly preferred for the American parties—could only be accomplished with a high level of organizational complexity. After all, they were not seeking well-organized parties for the sake of organization itself, but rather as a precondition for establishing parties that were more centralized and cohesive.

2   The codes and coding justifications for the British parties are available online at the website of the Political Science Department, Texas A&M University.

3   The codes used for producing the standardized placements of the parties cross-nationally for Figure 4.2 are slightly different than those reported in Table 4.1. The data in Table 4.1 were produced in the 1990s by coders at Texas A&M University for the Party Change Project (PCP), whose purpose was to generate *annual* codes for over-time comparisons within the United States and three other countries, including the United Kingdom. But in order to produce meaningful standardized scores, to place the U.S. and U.K. parties in a much broader comparative context, and to produce useful analyses of how parties' "environments" affect them ideologically, organizationally, and behaviorally, we need data for many more parties in a broader range of democracies than just the four that were included in the Party Change Project.

4   The entire ICPP sample includes 147 parties in 53 countries for the 1957–1962 period, including some that are noncompetitive parties and some in countries that are not democracies. Our "average z-scoring" procedures were actually used on that entire sample, of which the 95 competitive parties in 28 democracies constitute a significant subsample. The "mean" referred to here is the average of the scores for just the 95 competitive parties in 28 democracies.

5   While the bulk of Republican delegates are also now selected either directly or indirectly to reflect primary election results, the GOP leaves it up to the states to determine whether delegates will be bound to vote for particular candidates at the convention.

6   We should note that this chapter deals only with the distribution of power— and changes in that distribution—among the levels of party organization. It has not dealt with possible loss of power from the parties in general to outside

organizations. For instance, over time, the parties have lost some control over funding of the nomination process to political action committees. And for 2016, the GOP allowed Fox News to determine the parameters for who could participate in Republican presidential debates.

5 Cohesion
How Unified Are the Parties?

Party is a body of men united, for promoting by their joint endeavors the national interest, upon some particular principle in which they are all agreed.

(Edmund Burke 1770: 110)

Introduction

While Edmund Burke's definition might have seemed reasonable for parties of some type, some place, at some earlier time, it would certainly exclude the American parties of the twentieth and twenty-first centuries. "In which they are all agreed?" Those who associate with either of America's highly aggregative parties cannot be accused of "all agreeing" on much, if anything, of importance except the desire to win elections.

Although contemporary scholars recognize that parties vary in the degree of agreement on principles, they still recognize internal unity as one of the valued traits in a political party. French political scientist Jean Blondel (1978: 38) even cites "unity" as one of the four requirements of an *ideal* party. Unity is also preached in practical politics; witness the Preamble to the 1974 Charter of the Democratic Party: "We, the Democrats of the United States of America, united in common purposes, hereby rededicate ourselves to the principles which have historically sustained our Party."

The most important test of party unity in democratic politics comes when elected party members vote in legislatures. And although the APSA Committee stated other objectives as means to the end that it sought, it was ultimately most concerned about the level of cohesion within the parties in Congress. The Report saw the need for an *effective* party system, one that requires "first, that the parties are able to bring forth programs to which they commit themselves and, second, that the parties possess sufficient internal cohesion to carry out these programs" (APSA 1950: 1). This call for commitment to party programs and legislative cohesion in supporting the party program became the hallmark of the "responsible party" school of reformers. And particularly disconcerting to the

Committee, as included in the announced thesis of its Report, was that "historical and other factors" had caused the two parties to operate with "very little national cohesion" (APSA 1950: v). The Committee clearly felt that members of the two parties in the U.S. Congress had failed and were continuing to fail the "party unity" test.

Placing the U.S. and U.K. Parties Comparatively on Legislative Cohesion, 1950s

While party "cohesion," in its most abstract form, refers simply to the extent to which a party's representatives are unified when voting on legislation, the APSA Committee's concerns involved more than just that simplest version of cohesion. What the Committee envisioned were two internally cohesive parties that consistently voted *in opposition to one another*.

The *Congressional Quarterly* computes "party unity scores" as one way of measuring party cohesion on "party votes." A party unity score expresses the percentage of time that a member votes in agreement with a majority of his or her party on *party votes*, which are those that split the parties, when a majority of Democrats votes against a majority of Republicans. Aggregated over all party members in the House or the Senate, the mean party unity score is seen as an overall measure of cohesion within each party when party majorities take opposing stands. For the House of Representatives in the mid to late 1950s,[1] the average of these mean party unity scores was 71.3 for the Democrats and 69.8 for the Republicans. In the Senate, the scores averaged 68.8 for the Democrats and 69.0 for the Republicans. While some might regard such numbers as evidence of the parties being relatively cohesive, it is important to remember that a representative who voted merely by flipping a coin would be on his or her party's side 50 percent of the time. And when considering that the corresponding numbers would have been in the vicinity of 100 percent for the two British parties, the American parties' cohesion scores pale in comparison.

Another relevant point of comparison is the percentage of the time when legislative votes actually pit one unified party against the other. In other words, this indicator consists of the percentage of the time that legislative votes are actually "party votes." In the United Kingdom, after all, not only were the Labour and Conservative parties unified within themselves, but they also made it clear—every time divisions of the house were taken—how the one party differed from the other. Virtually all members of the "government party" voted for the government's policies, and virtually all members of the "opposition party" voted against those policies. The average voter needed to know only which party was in government (i.e., had a majority of seats in the House of Commons) to know which party was responsible for all legislation that was passed.

Congressional Quarterly has, since 1946, produced simple counts of these "party votes," when the majorities in the two parties are voting against one another. While in the United Kingdom it may have been reasonable to report the percentage of the time when 90 percent or more of the Labour Party voted against 90 percent or more of the Conservative Party, which happened on nearly all divisions of the house, that threshold was crossed so infrequently in the United States as to make it nearly meaningless as a measure of party voting.[2] But during much of the 1940s and early 1950s, even the substantially lower threshold of "simple majority of one party versus simple majority of the other party" was crossed less than a majority of the time in the House of Representatives.[3]

So as compared to their British counterparts at roughly the time that the APSA Committee was writing or had just written its Report, both American parties in Congress were relatively lacking not only in internal party cohesion, but also in voting in ways that would sharply differentiate their policy orientations—and responsibility—for the electorate.

Broader Comparison

While using measures of cohesion or party-line voting based on "party votes" makes sense for two-party systems, it is not relevant to multiparty systems, where legislative voting does not involve just one party voting against one other party. So in order to put the U.S. and U.K. parties in broader comparative perspective, involving cases of both two-party and multiparty systems, it is necessary to use a different type of measure.

The information presented in Figure 5.1 is based on more direct measurement of party cohesion in general, not just party cohesion on party votes. The index of cohesion is simply the size of the difference between the percentage of a party's members voting "yes" and the percentage voting "no" when a legislative vote is taken. The measure ranges from 0.0 in the case of a party splitting 50/50 in supporting/opposing a bill, to 1.0 in the case of all its members voting on the same side. A party's level of cohesion is simply its average index of cohesion for all votes in the analysis.

For our study, the major difficulty in measuring party cohesion across a range of countries results from the fact that the literature on political parties rarely reports precise indices of cohesion for legislative voting. When we knew the actual numbers voting yes and no on legislative votes, we calculated the index of cohesion. In the complete absence of such data, party cohesiveness was estimated as shown in the table on p. 76.

Even after resorting to estimating party cohesion from statements in the literature, we found that some parties still could not be coded because of inadequate information. However, it was possible to score 70 parties for this analysis. Because these scores tended to bunch up at the high end of the scale, we created some separation between them for Figure 5.1 by squaring the actual cohesion scores. Countries whose parties had the

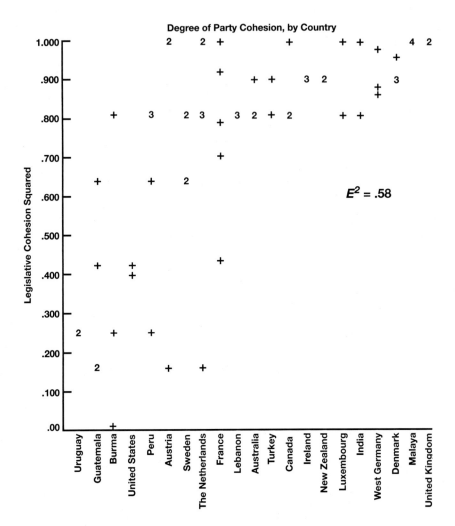

Figure 5.1 Degree of Party Cohesion, Averaged by Country
Source: Harmel and Janda (1982: 84)

Descriptive Statement	Divisions	Estimated Index
Completely cohesive	100/0	1.00
Highly cohesive	90/10	.80
Somewhat cohesive	80/20	.60
Not cohesive	70/30	.40
Divisive	60/40	.20
Highly divisive	50/50	.00

highest levels of cohesion included Malaya, Denmark, West Germany,[4] and, not surprisingly, the United Kingdom. At the other end, countries whose parties had the lowest cohesion included Uruguay, Guatemala, Burma, and, equally unsurprisingly, the United States. Most importantly for analysis of the U.S. parties, it is very clear that they were not only lacking in cohesion relative to their British counterparts, but were also markedly less cohesive than most competitive parties in the world's democracies at that time.

Why the U.S. and U.K. Parties Were So Different on Legislative Cohesion

As with decentralization of power, the APSA's Committee had it right in their assumption regarding the relative levels of cohesion in the American parties as contrasted from the British. The U.K. parties were indeed highly cohesive, and the American parties were highly incohesive. Part of the explanation can certainly be found in the significantly different governmental structures of the two countries. In earlier cross-national analysis, Harmel and Janda (1982) drew upon existing structural/institutional explanations for varying levels of cohesion across democracies' parties, and found that one such factor—the relationship between the executive and the legislature—could alone explain a substantial amount of the variation in party cohesion.

Where the executive and the legislators are separately elected, as in America's presidential form of government, the executive leadership does not depend on party unity in the legislature. In parliamentary systems such as Great Britain's, on the other hand, the executive is selected by the parliament and depends on continued support from the parliamentary majority. This puts a premium on party unity, so much so that effective "tools of discipline" are forged to assure such unity.[5] As a general rule, party cohesion is lower in presidential systems than in parliamentary systems.[6] With direct relevance for the U.S.–U.K. comparison, Ozbudun (1970: 363) argued that "parliamentary government is a sufficiently strong factor to produce cohesive legislative parties, provided that it operates in a two-party or moderate two-party system" (see Box 5.1).

Indeed, critics of the responsible party model of programmatic and cohesive parties have often argued that the American political environment is not conducive to such parties. They have specifically noted that cohesive parties are the products of parliamentary systems and their demand for party unity to keep governments in power, while the American presidential system allows the president to serve a four-year term regardless of defeats in congressional voting. That argument has been supported by evidence from Harmel and Janda's earlier analysis, which found that party cohesion did tend to be very low in presidential systems, especially as compared

Box 5.1 Presidential vs. Parliamentary Systems

In a democratic presidential system such as exists in the United States:

- The effective "head of government"—the president—is elected "by the people" (either directly or indirectly through an electoral college) in his or her own election, and is *not* elected by the national legislature.
- The president holds office for an entire fixed term (in the United States: four years) even when the majority(ies) of seats in one or both houses of Congress may be held by the other party, making it difficult for the president to get legislative support for his or her programs.
- The legislators are selected independently of the president for their own fixed terms, which they will be allowed to complete without fear of the president calling for early elections.

In a Westminster-style parliamentary system such as exists in the United Kingdom:

- The chief executive or "head of government"—usually called the "prime minister"—is selected by the legislature.
- The head of government holds his or her office as long as there is majority support for the executive's programs in the legislature. When the executive loses on a "vote of no confidence" in parliament, the cabinet resigns and calls for new elections.
- The head of government can dissolve parliament at any time and can call for new elections.

to the much higher cohesion that was normally found in parliamentary systems.

But other evidence suggests that higher levels of party cohesion are possible, even in presidential systems. In fact, higher cohesion was the case in the United States itself at an earlier time. The study of party cohesion in Congress from 1886 to 1966 by Brady et al. (1979: 384–385, 393) found that party voting was highest in the 1890–1910 period and lowest in the period 1940–1966. The mean cohesion for the Democrats for 1890–1910 was .74, compared to .65 for the period 1940–1966. The Republican cohesion dropped from .78 to .68 over the same period. Even when cohesion was higher in the congressional parties of the United States, though, it was still far lower than what has commonly been seen in the parliamentary parties of Great Britain.

Box 5.2 The Risky Business of Party Discipline in the U.S. Congress

Though the American party leaders' toolboxes for punishing wayward members of Congress are not completely empty, the few tools that exist are seldom used and, even then, are generally ineffective.

When national party leaders have occasionally attempted to affect nominations for congressional seats by campaigning against problematic incumbents during the nomination process, it has generally not gone well. The most famous instance was President Franklin Roosevelt's "purge attempt" of 1938, when he supported alternatives to a number of Southern Democratic incumbents. As reported by William Keefe and Morris Ogul (2001: 116), FDR's action "ended in disaster, with nearly all of the victims singled out for elimination winning handily." The takeaway seemed clear: Americans tend to view members of Congress as local representatives and congressional nominations as local business in which the influence of national party figures is unwelcome.

Another tool of punishment that has been used, though rarely, is withdrawal of an important committee assignment within Congress. Such was the case when the House Democrats punished one of their members in 1983 for what was seen as an "extreme case" of party disloyalty. Representative Phil Gramm of Texas had previously been an economics professor, and relished his seat on the House Budget Committee. But Gramm's thoughts on economic matters were more in line with those of President Ronald Reagan, a Republican, than with those of Gramm's fellow Democrats on the Committee. As reported by Janda et al. (1987: 222):

> Gramm began to meet with Reagan's director of the Office of Management and Budget . . . to reveal the Democrats' plans and to devise an alternative budget for 1982. Word soon leaked out, and several Democratic members of the Budget Committee objected to Gramm's participation in their meetings. The chairman of the House Democratic Caucus described Gramm as "the fox in the hen house."

Gramm not only stopped meeting with his Democratic colleagues, but he met instead with Republicans on the Committee and went on to co-sponsor the Republicans' alternative to the Democrats' budget proposal.

After Gramm was re-elected to another term as a Democrat in 1982, his party's leadership sought to settle the score by keeping him from being reappointed to the Budget Committee. Normally, parties don't punish their members for simply voting against the party's line; nearly every member would have to be punished if that were the case. But Gramm's behavior was seen as extreme, and punishment was brought to bear.

The ultimate consequence, though, was hardly what the party leadership had intended. After being denied reappointment to the Budget Committee as a Democrat, Gramm resigned his congressional seat and announced he would seek election again as a Republican. In the subsequent special election, Gramm not only won his seat back as a Republican, but was then made a Republican appointee to the Budget Committee. The Democrats had brought discipline to bear on one of their members, only to have it backfire.

While such experiences have kept the parties from using disciplinary tools on a regular basis, they have not completely stopped the practice. Beginning after the 2012 election, for instance, the House Republican leadership embarked on a limited "punishment" strategy that ultimately led to a number of disciplinary actions. Though any backlash was not as dramatic as that encountered by the Democrats in Gramm's case, in at least one instance (removal of Congressman Mark Meadows from a subcommittee chairmanship) the Republican leadership did an embarrassing, almost immediate about-face after protests by other Tea Party members. A headline dated June 24, 2015, and stating "Boehner Endorses Punishment for GOP Dissenter," was followed by one on June 25, 2015, declaring, "GOP Leaders Reverse Punishment for Dissenter" (see notes 10 and 11 for more detail).

Legislative Cohesion in the U.S. Parties Today

In Chapter 1, we noted that the APSA Committee assumed better organization and greater nationalization of party power would be necessary preconditions for increasing the levels of cohesion in the American parties. Centralization would hardly be possible without strong organization at the national level, and centralization would presumably be necessary in order to produce greater discipline in Congress. Without greater discipline, the tools for which already existed in the highly cohesive British parties, what hope would there be for increased cohesion in the U.S.?

In the previous chapters on organization and decentralization, we found that the American parties had changed only modestly on those two dimensions between the time of the Committee's observations and today, in spite of seemingly relevant changes in their environments. Following the presumed logic of the Committee's Report, then, it would clearly be expected that the relatively low levels of cohesion would remain as well. And yet, there is ample evidence for concluding that the American congressional parties are markedly more cohesive—and more partisan— now than when the Committee was doing its work in the late 1940s[7] (see Figures 5.2 and 5.3). The percentage of House roll calls involving party unity votes, where a majority of one party voted against the majority of the other party, has generally been substantially higher over the past few decades (averaging 55.1 percent for 1991–2012) than it was for most of the 1940s (averaging 46.9 percent for 1941–1950). (The trend is even more apparent in the dashed line of Figure 5.2, where "consensus votes" are removed.[8]) And again, the average percentage of the time that House members have voted with their parties' majorities has been markedly higher since the 1990s (88.6 percent for 1991–2012) than was the case in

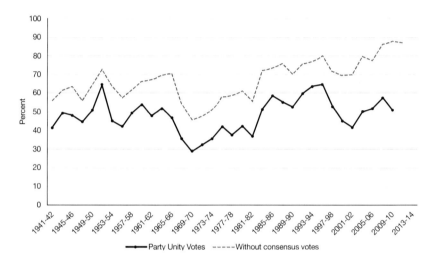

Figure 5.2 Party Unity Votes in the House

Source: Ornstein et al. (2014) and Bond and Smith (2016)

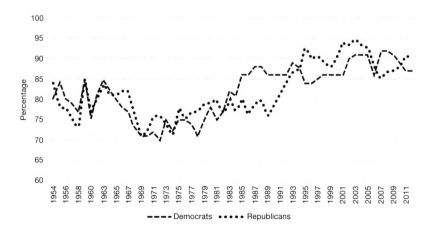

Figure 5.3 Party Cohesion in the House

Source: Ornstein et al. (2014)

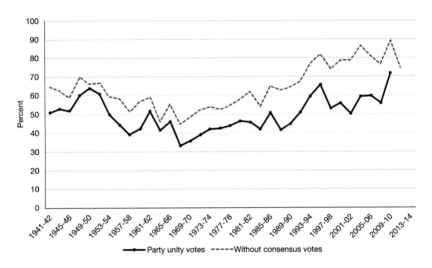

Figure 5.4 Party Unity Votes in the Senate
Source: Ornstein et al. (2014) and Bond and Smith (2016)

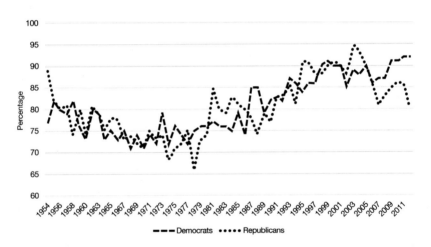

Figure 5.5 Party Cohesion in the Senate
Source: Ornstein et al. (2014)

the 1950s–1970s (77.2 percent for 1954–1979).[9] Similar tendencies are apparent for the Senate (see Figures 5.4 and 5.5).

Given the relatively smaller changes that we found for organizational complexity and decentralization of power, it would seem that the much more substantial changes in level of cohesion could not be credited to other structural changes in the parties themselves. And given that the United

States has maintained a presidential system throughout the periods we are comparing here, today's higher cohesion scores could hardly be attributed to significant institutional change involving the relationship of executive and legislature. Additionally, it would certainly be hard to substantiate any claim that the parties themselves produced the greater cohesion by means of more effective implementation of party discipline. A strategy of limited "punishment" was pursued by House Republican leadership beginning in 2012,[10] but that occurred years after the party was already producing the higher level of cohesion. And the higher levels of cohesion for Republicans in the Senate and Democrats in both houses had also occurred without increased use of party discipline. Instead, we have to look elsewhere to explain the dramatically higher levels of cohesion that we have observed in recent decades, as compared to the situation that the APSA Committee had just experienced.

There can be little doubt that one contributing factor was the dramatic change in partisan voting behavior in the South. For decades, the Democratic Party reigned supreme in the South, not just in local elections, but in congressional elections as well. As the APSA Committee was considering what to put in its Report, the 1948 session of the House of Representatives included 103 Democrats from the South, and only two Republicans. Many of those Southern Democrats thought and voted quite differently (i.e., much more conservatively) than their fellow Democrats from the North, thus contributing to relatively low cohesion among the Democrats as a whole. But then came the Voting Rights Act of 1964 and a consequential shift in the voting behavior of many Southern voters; no longer satisfied to cast their votes for conservative Democrats, they voted instead for Republicans. By 1972, the Southern distribution of House seats was 73 Democrats to 34 Republicans. The Democrats maintained this much-reduced advantage of 30–50 Southern seats through 1992. Then came the "earthquake election" of 1994, with Republicans claiming 64 seats to the Democrats' 61, and the pattern of Democratic dominance in the South had officially come to an end. Since then, the South has consistently produced a Republican House seat advantage, never falling below 17 seats and peaking (so far) at 63 seats in 2014. The result—from the standpoint of cohesion within the Democratic Party—would naturally be a more cohesive set of House members. What had been a regionally divided party was now a more unified, more solidly "northern" aggregation.

At roughly the same time, partisan voting in New England was going through a similar transformation. This time, though, it was the Republicans who had traditionally enjoyed a significant edge in House voting. When the APSA Committee members were observing the 80th Congress (1948–1949), for instance, Republicans held 21 of the 28 House seats from New England. Even "liberals" had to run as Republicans in order to win in New England, and some did, thus contributing to relatively low cohesion scores for the Republican Party nationally. But by the 1960s, some of those liberal Republicans would be replaced by Democrats, with Republicans assuming minority status within the New England delegation. And by the 2008 election, the entire delegation was Democratic. The consequence for cohesion in the Republican Party: with the New England liberals gone, the remainder of the party was naturally more cohesive (see Box 5.3).

So, some—and perhaps much—of the increased cohesion within congressional parties can ultimately be attributed to regional changes in voters' behavior, resulting in two parties whose representatives would just "naturally" be more alike in their thinking and their legislative behavior. But while we have already suggested that this had taken place in the absence of greater *party* discipline,[11] we would be remiss not to note the possible additional influence recently of greater discipline being exerted from *outside* the party, at least for the Republicans.

The very high cohesion scores for Republicans in both houses since 2009 might be partly explained by pressure being brought by the right-wing Tea Party movement. Formed in response to the Democratic Administration's

---

Box 5.3 A Partisan Sea Change in New England

In 2008, the year Barack Obama was first elected President, Republican Congressman Christopher Shays from Connecticut lost the House seat he had held for nine consecutive terms to a political newcomer, Democrat Jim Himes. Shay's loss marked something of a turning point in New England history. As put by Peter Appelbome (2008: A26):

> When [Christopher Shays] went to Congress in 1987, he was one of nine Republican representatives from the six New England states. Now there are none. He inherited a seat long held by independent-minded Republicans . . . [and] he was part of a tradition of Northeastern moderates . . .

As noted in Appelbome's article, Shays himself attributed part of his and the GOP's difficulties in the northeast to his party's lack of diversity and its emphasis on social conservatism.

Though there have again, since Shays' departure, been Republicans from New England in the House, the general tendency noted in the article has not been significantly challenged. In 2010, two Republicans were elected to the House, both from New Hampshire. After the 2012 election, New England's representation was again 100 percent Democrats. In 2014, two Republicans went to the House, one from Maine and one from New Hampshire.

stimulus program, the movement has achieved significant impact, not only by identifying enthusiastic representatives—many of whom are virtually fearless due to residing in safe, gerrymandered districts—but also through its threats to mount well-funded and well-organized nomination challenges to Republican incumbents who dare to ignore its demands. Adding weight to the threats were some notable Tea Party successes: incumbent Senator Bob Bennett losing his state convention bid for re-nomination to Tea Party'er Mike Lee, and longtime incumbent Richard Lugar losing to primary challenger and Tea Party-backed Richard Murdock (who ultimately lost the seat in the general election).[12] Similar pressures were applied on the House side. Representative Bob Inglis (SC –4) was defeated in a 2010 primary by Tea Party'er Trey Gowdy, after Inglis had supported the federal bailout in 2008 (and had previously refused to support the Iraq War surge in 2007). Some of the more moderate Republicans for whom the threat of a Tea Party challenge allegedly played some role in deciding not to run for re-election include Senators Kay Bailey Hutchinson (TX; replaced by Ted Cruz) and Olympia Snow[13] (ME), who had voted in favor of President Obama's healthcare package. The net result of the Tea Party-engineered replacements—and the threats of more replacements—was undoubtedly even greater cohesion among Republicans than would have been accomplished by the New England realignment alone.

The Tea Party's effectiveness in employing discipline from outside the party actually stands as strong testimony of the Republican Party's own inability to employ discipline from within. Rather than the GOP leaders threatening discipline toward staunch right-wing members who refused to follow the leaders' more moderate approach, the party leaders themselves were forced to yield in the face of Tea Party directives. In 2013, with some moderate members overtly fearful of an anti-Republican backlash from the public, the majority of the party in the House still voted to "shut down" the government in an effort to kill Obamacare, though only a minority of the caucus—and scarcely any of the leadership—were personally enthusiastic about the strategy. While the writers of the APSA Committee's Report may have looked to development of stronger leadership as a means of forging greater party unity, the fact is that the relatively greater unity that exists within the House GOP today does so in spite of weak leadership. In today's GOP, congressional leaders are well aware that a combination of Tea Party-backed representatives and others threatened by Tea Party challenges could presumably dictate a change in leadership at any time. Indeed, in the face of such a challenge, Speaker John Boehner chose to resign from the position rather than fight to keep it (see Box 5.4).

It is noteworthy, in any case, that the major factions of the Republican Party today differ not only ideologically, but even more so on strategic grounds. The bottom line, ideologically, is that virtually all Republican members of Congress today are "conservative," and certainly more conservative than virtually all of the Democrats, as distinguished from the

---

Box 5.4 Why Being Speaker Ain't What It Used to Be

On January 1, 2013, John Boehner was re-elected to his second term as Speaker of the House of Representatives. In an article that appeared in the *Washington Post*'s blog *The Fix*, Chris Cillizza gave "5 reasons why being Speaker of the House ain't what it used to be." "The Speakership is at (or near) its low ebb in terms of raw power," Cilliza argued, "thanks to a combination of changing rules in the House and the emerging political realities." Boehner was being asked to lead a House torn "by broad ideological divides—both between the parties and within the GOP—and by a new class of Republicans who viewed compromise as a dirty word."

Cilliza's "five reasons" included an earmarking ban that effectively removed an important tool from the Speaker's arsenal, politics and ideology having trumped loyalty, more opportunities for members to develop their own bases of power, weaker political parties, and lack of job security.

When Boehner was again elected to the Speakership in 2015, the "5 reasons" were still very much applicable. So much so, in fact, that less than halfway through the new term—in the midst of a serious challenge to his leadership—Boehner resigned as Speaker (and as a member of the House) on October 30, 2015.

---

earlier times when liberal Republicans could be more liberal than conservative Democrats. What divides the Tea Party conservatives from the Wall Street conservatives is not so much their relative conservatism, but rather their differences over how best to accomplish their ideological goals. Whereas Tea Party'ers may be willing to shut down all of federal government as a tactic in achieving their policy goals, Wall Street conservatives favor accomplishing many of the same goals by using more traditional means (i.e., the legislative process). It has been only rarely—as in the cases of voting on Hurricane Sandy relief (late January 2013) or raising the debt ceiling and adopting a continuing resolution with the effect of reopening government (October 2013)—that the public has been overtly aware of the GOP's strategic split. On such occasions—when potential catastrophes are perceived for the party and/or the country—the final vote tallies (especially in the House) make clear that the Republicans are not so united on everything. But the rest of the time, their legislative voting behavior reveals that they can be united on most things—at least, on many more than would have been the case in the 1940s or 1950s.[14]

Indeed, if the APSA Committee thought that the parties would have to be better organized and more centralized in order to be more cohesive, they would certainly be discouraged today to learn (from Chapters 3 and 4) that the parties were already well organized back then, and that they have become only marginally more centralized over time. But just as they might be discouraged, they would certainly be amazed to find that the parties have, somehow, still become significantly more cohesive over the past few decades. Rather than embarking on a path of greater party discipline as a means of forcing party unity,[15] the American parties took a different route that led them toward the same objective. The first and most significant factor was a change in voting behavior in the South and in New England, effectively ridding the Democrats of southern conservatives and the Republicans of northeastern liberals, thereby resulting in groups of Democratic and Republican representatives who are just naturally "more alike" within their respective parties. But the story—at least for the Republicans—doesn't end there. Discipline from outside the party—at the hands of the Tea Party movement and its confederates—has effectively forged even greater cohesion within the party.

Regardless of how they have gotten there, the American parties have achieved—at least to some degree—the greater cohesion that the APSA Committee desired.

Box 5.5 U.S. Party Cohesion in Current Comparative Perspective

In February 2014, political scientist David W. Brady wrote a brief article for the *Washington Post*'s *Monkey Cage* blog titled "Sure, Congress Is Polarized. But Other Legislatures Are More So." The article makes clear that while the American parties are more polarized and cohesive today than previously, they would still have a far distance to travel before reaching the levels of cohesion that is found in many parliamentary democracies.

When applying a standard measure of unified party voting (the "Rice index," with maximum score of 100) to 90 parties in 16 Western parliamentary democracies, Brady reported the lowest score being 88.63, with an average over 97. "In contrast," he noted, ". . . over time in the U.S. Congress, the index's high score is 66 and, even when adjusted, is in the 75 range." His conclusion: Congress does not seem particularly polarized when compared to parliamentary systems.

Projects and Exercises

Project 5.1: Survey of Attitudes on Party Unity in Congress

In Project 2.3 of Chapter 2, you have already been introduced to Jack Dennis's survey of Americans' attitudes toward their political parties in 1964.

In addition to the questions pertaining to how much "choice" the respondents would have preferred the parties to provide on the issues, Dennis also asked questions about their attitudes regarding how much members of Congress should feel compelled to follow their party leaders' preferences and to work together with the majority of their party in Congress. Dennis found that when asked whether "Our senators and representatives ought to follow their party leaders more than they do," 41 percent agreed and 33 percent disagreed (with the rest undecided). But when asked about the more specific statement, "A senator or representative should follow his party leaders even if he doesn't want to," only 23 percent agreed and 63 percent disagreed.

What do you suppose explains the difference in the responses to those two questions?

_____

_____

_____

_____

To the more abstract statement, "We would be better off if all the Democrats in government stood together and all the Republicans did the same," 32 percent agreed and 54 percent disagreed.

Unfortunately, as we noted earlier about Dennis's findings pertaining to "party choice," there has been no subsequent report of later surveys that asked the same questions Dennis asked about Members of Congress following the lead of their party. So while we know what some Americans felt in the 1960s, we don't know what Americans might feel today.

Though it would not be possible for you alone to survey a large enough group of American citizens to produce a scientifically valid study, it would nonetheless be interesting to know how your family and friends feel about the degree to which Members of Congress should follow their party's lead today.

With your instructor's help, design and implement a questionnaire that includes at least the three questions listed below:

Do you agree or disagree with the following statement? "A senator or representative should follow his or her party leaders even if he or she doesn't want to."

Circle one: Agree / Disagree / Neither Agree nor Disagree / Don't Know

Do you agree or disagree with the following statement? "We would be better off if all the Democrats in government stood together and all the Republicans did the same."

Circle one: Agree / Disagree / Neither Agree nor Disagree / Don't Know

Do you agree or disagree with the following statement? "Our senators and representatives ought to follow their party leaders more than they do."

Circle one: Agree / Disagree / Neither Agree nor Disagree / Don't Know

Exercise 5.1: Impact of Partisan Change in the South

Since 1950, *Congressional Quarterly* has been keeping track of voting behavior within the Congress. Among the statistics they have produced on a regular basis are lists of members who have been most and least supportive of their own parties' majorities when voting on legislation.

In Appendix C, you will find the "top 20" lists of Democratic *opposers* in the House of Representatives for every decennial year from 1950 to 2010. The "percentage opposition" score for each Congressman is the percentage of the time that the member voted against a majority of his or her party's members in the House.

Compute the percentage of those House members in each top 20 list who were from southern states (using the 11 formerly Confederate states as the southern states: South Carolina, Mississippi, Florida, Alabama, Georgia, Louisiana, Texas, Virginia, Arkansas, Tennessee, and North Carolina), and complete Table 5.1. What pattern is obvious from studying that row of the table?

Next, compute the average percentage of opposition across the 20 members on each of the lists. Use those numbers to complete Table 5.2. What pattern is evident from studying that row of the table?

Table 5.1 Percentage of Top Democratic "Opposers" from the South

	1950	1960	1970	1980	1990	2000	2010
(% from southern states)	___	___	___	___	___	___	___

Table 5.2 Degree of "In-Party Opposition" from Top Democratic Opposers

	1950	1960	1970	1980	1990	2000	2010
(average % opposition)	___	___	___	___	___	___	___

Exercise 5.2: Party Cohesion and Parliamentary vs. Presidential Systems

As discussed above, there are differences between parliamentary and presidential systems of government that seemingly bear directly on parties' need for legislative cohesion. In parliamentary systems, where control of the executive depends structurally on support from the party's legislators, loyalty to the party is critically important. This is not so much the case for presidential systems, where presidents and the legislators have their own fixed terms of office and where party cohesion is helpful but not essential for governing.

In the data set of Appendix B, you will find the data necessary to "test" the expectation that parties in countries with parliamentary systems are more likely to be cohesive (*cohesion*) than are the parties in countries with presidential systems (*presparl*). The first thing we note is the scarcity of presidential systems in our sample. In fact, there are relatively few presidential systems in democracies worldwide. The four that are found in our sample are the United States, Guatemala, Peru, and Uruguay. Those four countries account for 13 of the 70 parties for which we have data on party cohesion.

In the table below, enter the number of parties that qualify for each cell. For instance, in the upper left-hand cell, put the number of parties that are "low in cohesion" and are also found in presidential countries. In the upper right-hand cell, put the number of parties that are "low in cohesion" and are also found in parliamentary countries, and so on. After these "frequencies" are placed in all four boxes, add up the numbers in the first column (upper and lower left-hand cells) and put the total on the blank line under that column. Do similarly for the right-hand column. Then divide each of the cell frequencies by its column frequency, and put that percentage in the cell, along with the cell frequency you have already placed there. Do this for all four cells. You now have what you need to do "cross-tabulation analysis." In other words, you have what you need to see whether there is any support for our expectation that countries with presidential systems are more likely than countries with parliamentary systems to produce parties with a relatively low level of cohesion.

	Presidential System	**Parliamentary System**
Low cohesion		
Hi cohesion		

_____   _____

Compare the percentage in the upper left-hand cell to the percentage in the upper right-hand cell. Is the percentage in the left-hand cell substantially larger than the percentage in the right-hand cell? _____ If so, then our expectation is supported by the data.

Notes

1 *Congressional Quarterly* reported these scores beginning for the 1956 session of Congress. The average scores reported here cover the years 1956–1959. For the actual scores, see http://media.cq.com/log/2013/01/vote-studies/.

2 This remained true until at least the 1990s, when the percentage of votes on which the 90 percent vs. 90 percent threshold was met began increasing substantially in both houses. It is unlikely, however, that this had occurred more than 50 percent of the time in any session through the time of the writing of this book.

3 Based on information from Figure 7.2 of Stanley and Niemi (1990: 194).

4 We should note that for Greece we have information on cohesion for just one of the four Greek parties in the data set, and that party had a very high cohesion score. Some of the other countries are also represented here by fewer than their total numbers of parties in our sample; some of the parties have "missing data" for cohesion. Another country where this reduces the number of parties to just one (from three) is Uganda. Thus, the placements for the "averages" for those two countries (based on just one case each), in particular, might be viewed with some caution, and hence we have not included them in Figure 5.1.

5 In the United Kingdom, for instance, the ultimate tool for discipline is the "withdrawal of the whip," which ultimately means the expulsion of the member from the party. Though used very rarely to punish members for voting against the party's position, it is still thought to enhance discipline simply by remaining in the party's arsenal; members know that it could be used.

6 As put by William Galston (2010), "Judged by parliamentary standards, the American party system is bound to appear defective."

7 The Committee on Political Parties was created by the American Political Science Association at its annual meeting in 1946.

8 The dashed line still reflects "party unity votes," but now excluding consensus votes—where less than 10 percent of the entire House constitute the minority—from the analysis. The revised numbers can be interpreted as the percentage of all conflict on the House and Senate floor that is actually partisan conflict. The number of consensus votes—which include "ceremonial" bills on things such as naming of federal buildings—increased markedly beginning in the 1960s. The data excluding the ceremonial votes were created by Jon Bond; we thank him for providing them—and their interpretation—to us.

9 Unfortunately we cannot report comparable figures for the 1940s, since *Congressional Quarterly* has computed these scores only for congressional sessions beginning with 1954.

10 While reorganizing after the 2012 election, the Steering Committee of the House Republicans chose not to reassign four members to important committee assignments they had held previously; in all cases, these were perceived as acts of punishment. After the 2014 election, two members who had served on the Rules Committee were not reassigned to that important post. In 2015, three members who had served on the Republican whip team were removed from those positions after voting against the leadership's wishes on rules pertaining to an important trade bill. Another member voting against the trade bill itself was stripped of a subcommittee chairmanship, but was almost immediately reinstated after protests from fellow Tea Party'ers.

11 See endnote 10 concerning recent disciplinary efforts by the House Republican leadership. Those efforts obviously would not have affected the increases in

cohesion that had already occurred earlier, nor the changes that have occurred in the cohesion levels of Senate Republicans and Democrats in both houses.

12 Murkowski (AK) also lost to a Tea Party-backed primary challenger. However, she then ran as an independent and was re-elected in the general election; she still caucuses with the GOP.

13 Snowe announced that her decision to retire was based on unhappiness with the growing partisanship in the Senate, but that decision followed the announced decision of the Tea Party Express to support any conservative challenger (*Roll Call*, February 10, 2011).

14 It may seem odd to reference the "factionalism" within the Republican Party at the same time that we note its greater behavioral "unity" over time. Hence, we should make clear that it is possible for a party that is factionalized in leadership and even policy preferences to still be united in opposition to the other party when voting on legislation.

15 On more recent disciplinary efforts of House Republican leadership, see notes 10 and 11.

6   Conclusion

Voting and Governing with More "Responsible" Parties

> There is no constitutional mechanism for solving disputes between the executive and the legislature. That wasn't such a problem when the parties weren't particularly polarized . . ., but it's a huge and growing problem in an age when the parties loathe each other.
>
> (Ezra Klein 2015)

Since publication of the APSA Committee's Report in 1950, the parties have moved in the direction of some of its specific recommendations but have ignored or moved in the opposite direction on others, as indicated in Table 6.1. Regardless of that particular "report card," though, we have noted in previous chapters that there has been significant movement on some of the Committee's broader goals, whether deliberately or unintentionally. Most importantly, the two major parties have developed more distinctive policy profiles and have become more cohesive in their legislative behavior.

Though the APSA Committee's main focus of attention was the American *parties*, the ultimate objective was to develop parties that would be more useful for *voters*. The committee's main objectives for the parties—that they should make clearer how their policy programs differed from one another, and then effectively force their government representatives to toe their respective party lines—were not meant to achieve stronger parties just for the sake of having stronger parties. Rather, the intention was to provide voters the opportunity—which British voters presumably had already—to know how the parties' candidates would behave (differently) when voting on legislation, simply by knowing the candidates' party affiliations.

But that "model" was based on an important premise: that the American voting public would actually have welcomed more *ideological* parties (i.e., parties that would have taken clearer—and more clearly different—ideological stances). In reality, the evidence suggests that American citizens as of the 1960s (the earliest time period for which clear data exist) had, at best, mixed views on how "different" they wanted the parties to be. A study of Wisconsin voters (Dennis 1966), based on a 1964 survey,

Table 6.1 APSA Committee Recommendations: Current Status*

Recommendations	Current Status (2015)
Ideology	
Create Party Council to adopt and interpret platforms	No
Platforms adopted every two years	No
Organization	
National conventions held every two years	No[1]
Fewer delegates and alternatives at national conventions	Opposite direction; both have gotten larger
Convention delegates apportioned by party strength in states	Partly so in both parties
National Committee maintains national party headquarters	Both
National Committee raises adequate funding	Both
Larger permanent professional staffs for national committees	Both
Candidate nominations made in closed primaries	Neither party requires closed primaries
More pre-primary conventions	No
Decentralization	
National convention more active in selection of National Committee members	No
National Committee members reflect party strength areas they represent	Partly so for Democrats; no for Republicans
Create Party Council to make recommendations about congressional candidates	No
Create Party Council to discipline state/local parties deserting national platform	No
Require state platforms to be adopted after national platform	No
State and local platforms made to conform to the national platform	No
Adopt a national presidential primary	No

continued . . .

Table 6.1 Continued

Recommendations	Current Status (2015)
Cohesion	
Make platforms binding on all party officeholders at all levels	No
Members of Congress to participate more actively in platform-writing	No
Consolidate all House and Senate leadership positions into one committee	No
Parties hold more frequent congressional caucus/conference meetings	Yes for Republicans; opposite for Democrats[2]
Caucus/conference decisions on legislative policy are finding on Members of Congress	No
No committee chairmanships by seniority for opponents of party programs	No
Replace Rules Committee control of the legislative calendar with leadership control	Indirectly[3]

* Table entries adopted/adapted from Ranney (1973) and Green and Herrnson (2002).
1 The option to hold conventions every two years is included in the Democratic Party's Charter adopted at a midterm convention in 1974. The party held additional midterm conventions in 1978 and 1982 but has not done so since then.
2 See Forgette (2004).
3 Technically, the Rules Committee still controls the calendar, but the leadership controls the Rules Committee.

reported that 54 percent agreed with the statement that "The parties do more to confuse the issues than to provide a clear choice on them," but only 31 percent agreed with the apparent solution: "Things would be better if the parties took opposite stands on issues more than they do now." Though the APSA Committee may have assumed that American voters would eagerly accept a change to more ideological parties, the survey evidence casts considerable doubt on that assumption.

The APSA model also assumed that the American citizenry would be welcoming of more disciplined—or at least more cohesive—political parties. Again, the same study of Wisconsin voters asked a number of relevant questions. While 41 percent of respondents agreed and only 33 percent disagreed that "Our senators and representatives ought to follow their party leaders more than they do," there was less agreement with the likely consequences of such behavior. Only 23 percent agreed (with 63 percent disagreeing) that "A senator or representative should follow his party leaders even if he doesn't want to," and just 30 percent agreed (with

54 percent disagreeing) that "We would be better off if all the Democrats in government stood together and all the Republicans did the same." It is not at all clear that following the APSA Committee's wishes would have been "good politics" for the American parties.

But regardless of what the American electorate *wanted*, a different question is whether they would have been prepared to act like "responsible citizens," in the mold of what the APSA Committee's model would require. If the parties actually did provide clearer choices on the issues, would the electorate have been capable of handling those choices in a rational manner? And even more to the Committee's point: would the voters have been sufficiently able to assimilate/internalize that information so as to accurately match their own issue preferences with those of the respective parties?

There is evidence that suggests that when the parties have provided clear choices on issues, the American voters have indeed been able to make effective use of that information. Using survey data for the 1964 electorate, one political scientist found that for the issues voters considered to be most "salient" to them, they could indeed perceive distinctions between the parties and could presumably use that information to help in making voting decisions (Repass 1971). A review of studies of voters "during periods of social and economic turmoil, when the policy options provided by the political parties tend to be relatively distinct," found that voters have used that party-based issue content to inform their votes (Carmines and Stimson 1980: 78). Others, using data over multiple elections from 1972 through 1996, have found that Americans have *increasingly* become better at distinguishing between the two parties on a range of issues across three dimensions (social welfare, racial, and cultural issues) (Layman and Carsey 2002), suggesting that as the parties have sent strong signals on their differences across a broadening array of issues, voters have been able to absorb and reflect that information. Indeed, there is evidence that American voters have increasingly sorted themselves into the "correct" parties, using ideological preferences.[1] Bottom line: the 1950 APSA Committee would presumably be pleased to find that when the parties do project clear differences on the issues, the American electorate is able to detect those differences, to accurately associate the parties with their positions, and to vote accordingly.

Earlier in the book, we have presented evidence that substantial headway has been made in homogenizing the meaning of the party labels, and thus making it easier for citizens to choose candidates and to hold representatives accountable simply by knowing their party affiliations. The "conservative southern Democrats" and "liberal New England Republicans," which were significant factions within their respective congressional parties in the 1940s and 1950s, are now a thing of the past. A Democrat in Congress—no matter what part of the country he or she represents—is much more likely to vote with the majority of other Democrats than was the case historically, and likewise for the Republican

Party. We have also reviewed evidence suggesting that since the writing of the Responsible Parties Report, the parties have increased in their ideological distinctiveness. Coupling those developments with the additional finding that the electorate understands the differences and can vote accordingly should certainly please the APSA Committee. Their ultimate goal, after all, was for the parties to provide clear differences on issues that the voters could perceive and use to make informed decisions, making it more easy and rational to vote (using just the party label), and then that the winners would act accordingly in their government positions. All who value voters being able to make rational voting decisions, based "on the issues" but using party labels as a guide, should also be pleased.

But the benefits that may have been realized in simplifying matters for the "voters" may actually have been offset by the realities associated with attempting to govern in the changed political environment.[2] The homogeneous parties—no longer the loose collections of regional/ideological tendencies that characterized both the Democrats and the Republicans at the time of the Report's writing—may have made for a more efficient policy-making milieu similar to that of parliamentary governments when the same party holds the White House and both houses of Congress, but have also contributed to gridlock when the president's party holds just one or neither of the two houses.[3] In a situation of divided government—which happens very frequently in the American system—presidents can no longer count on finding a sizable segment of the opposition party to join with the bulk of his or her own to forge a winning policy majority[4].

Box 6.1 In America, Polarization Is a Problem. In Britain, It Could Be a Solution.

Robert Ford, a Lecturer in Politics at the University of Manchester in the United Kingdom, is the author of an interesting, thought-provoking article (with the above title) that appeared in the *Washington Post*'s *Monkey Cage* blog on February 20, 2014. While many observers of American politics had been lamenting its growing polarization, in Britain—where inter-party differences had become increasingly more moderate—there were also reasons for concern.

Moderation had, Ford argued, "come at a cost, marginalizing those with more intense political views, and hollowing out the political parties' activist bases." And not only that! "The major parties' moderation has also sidelined real conflicts over economic inequality and social class without resolving them, leaving voters with the feeling that politicians are out of touch and unresponsive."

"In politics, everything comes with a price," Ford concludes. "Moderation is no exception."

Furthermore, under a system of homogeneity without party discipline—as has now developed in each party—it is increasingly difficult for the "leaders" of the branches and the parties to deliver on bipartisan deals, even when the will exists at the leadership level. And again, this is particularly apparent when government control is divided between the parties. On more than one occasion, President Obama and Speaker Boehner thought they had reached a "deal" only to have it fall apart when Boehner could not deliver his party's votes. While the homogeneity of purpose may exist within the party for broad ideological principles, the lack of discipline still means that members—individually or en bloc—can deviate from their leader's directions when/if they want to. Though the APSA Committee may have envisioned a system of two homogeneous American parties that would operate more like Britain's parliament, the lack of effective tools of party discipline means that when the executive and legislative powers are divided between two homogeneous parties with conflicting views (which can't happen in a parliamentary system), the separated powers are in some ways more separated than ever. And from the government's standpoint, that can and sometimes has meant virtual powerlessness to act.

Since the writing of the APSA Committee's report, important aspects of the context of American parties have changed so as to allow them to become more distinctive and more disciplined. But other important aspects of their environment—including in particular the executive-legislative arrangements—have not changed. The consequence is parties more like the British, attempting to operate in a very non-British governmental context, thus bringing a whole new set of challenges for the parties and would-be party reformers.[5]

Project

Project 6.1: Should We Really Want Responsible Parties?

Throughout the previous chapters of this book, we have noted that the APSA Committee was desirous of what we have come to call "responsible parties." Their desires were based on certain expectations of what parties—and parties' representatives in government—should do for voters and for those who are represented, more generally. The underlying assumption seemed to be that if given a choice, the average American citizen would choose more "responsible" parties rather than the more pragmatic parties they currently had. But is that necessarily the case? Consider what you value most about the American political system. Would parties such as those envisioned by the APSA Committee help or hinder your ability to maximize those things? Are there particular features of the responsible party model that would be helpful, while others might prove to be hindrances?

Notes

1   Haidt and Abrams (2015) report the relevant correlations between survey respondents' self-placements on a liberal-conservative continuum and their reported voting behavior by party. "If there were no relationship, the 'correlation coefficient' would be zero. If there were a perfect relationship, it would be 1. In 1972, it was 0.32, but it has nearly doubled since then, to 0.62 in 2012, which is considered strong."

2   Galston (2010), for instance, has reasoned that "the unending high-decibel partisan warfare of the past decade has led many Americans to look back with nostalgia on the more consensual if muddled party system that persisted until the 1970s."

3   The consequences of the increased polarization and resulting gridlock are deep and far-reaching. Moss (2012) argues, "it is threatening the nation's capacity to solve critical problems, from employment to energy to entitlements to education." Other potential consequences go to the heart of the American system of government. Klein (2015), for instance, argues that "as divided Congresses prove less able to govern, more and more domestic power will be claimed by the president." Klein also notes that "when governing majorities do exist, they will govern more aggressively."

4   Indeed, in their list of "The top 10 reasons American politics are so broken," Haidt and Abrams (2015) put "The two parties purified themselves ideologically" at the top of the list.

5   In his contemporaneous critique of the APSA Committee's Report, political scientist Austin Ranney (1951) reached a similar conclusion. As summarized by Thomas Mann (2015), "Ranney argued that more ideologically coherent, internally unified, and adversarial parties in the fashion of Westminster-style parliamentary democracy would be a disaster within the American constitutional system, because of its separation of powers, separately elected institutions, and constraints on majority rule that favor cross-party coalitions and compromise."

Appendix A

Toward a More Responsible Two-Party System: Summary and Conclusions[1]

SUMMARY OF CONCLUSIONS AND PROPOSALS

PART I. THE NEED FOR GREATER PARTY RESPONSIBILITY

1. The Role of the Political Parties

1. The Parties and Public Policy. Popular government in a nation of more than 150 million people requires political parties which provide the electorate with a proper range of choice between alternatives of action. In order to keep the parties apart, one must consider the relations between each and public policy. The reasons for the growing emphasis on public policy in party politics are to be found, above all; in the very operations of modern government.

2. The New Importance of Program. The crux of public affairs lies in the necessity for more effective formulation of general policies and programs and for better integration of all of the far-flung activities of modern government. It is in terms of party programs that political leaders can attempt to consolidate public attitudes toward the work plans of government.

3. The Potentialities of the Party System. The potentialities of the two-party system are suggested, on the one hand, by the fact that for all practical purposes the major parties monopolize elections, and, on the other, by the fact that both parties have in the past managed to adapt themselves to the demands made upon them by external necessities. It is good practical politics to reconsider party organization in the light of the changing conditions of politics. Happily such an effort entails an application of ideas about the party system that are no longer unfamiliar.

2. What Kind of Party System Is Needed?

The party system that is needed must be democratic, responsible and effective.

I. A Stronger Two-Party System

1. *The Need for an Effective Party System.* An effective party system requires, first, that the parties are able to bring forth programs to which they commit themselves and, second, that the parties possess sufficient internal cohesion to carry out these programs. Such a degree of unity within the parties cannot be brought about without party procedures that give a large body of people an opportunity to share in the development of the party program.

2. *The Need for an Effective Opposition Party.* The fundamental requirement of accountability is a two-party system in which the opposition party acts as the critic of the party in power, developing, defining and presenting the policy alternatives which are necessary for a true choice in reaching public decisions. The opposition most conducive to responsible government is an organized party opposition.

II. Better Integrated Parties

1. *The Need for a Party System with Greater Resistance to Pressure.* There is little to suggest that the phenomenal growth of interest organizations in recent decades has come to its end. The whole development makes necessary a reinforced party system that can cope with the multiplied organized pressures. Compromise among interests is compatible with the aims of a free society only when the terms of reference reflect an openly acknowledged concept of the public interest.

2. *The Need for a Party System with Sufficient Party Loyalty.* Needed clarification of party policy will not cause the parties to differ more fundamentally or more sharply than they have in the past. Nor is it to be assumed that increasing concern with their programs will cause the parties to erect between themselves an ideological wall. Parties have the right and the duty to announce the terms to govern participation in the common enterprise. The emphasis in all consideration of party discipline must be on positive measures to create a strong and general agreement on policies. A basis for party cohesion in Congress will be established as soon as the parties interest themselves sufficiently in their congressional candidates to set up strong and active campaign organizations in the constituencies.

III. More Responsible Parties

1. *The Need for Parties Responsible to the Public.* Party responsibility means the responsibility of both parties to the general public, as enforced in elections. Party responsibility to the public, enforced in elections, implies that there be more than one party, for the public

can hold a party responsible only if it has a choice. As a means of achieving responsibility, the clarification of party policy also tends to keep public debate on a more realistic level, restraining the inclination of party spokesmen to make unsubstantiated statements and charges.

2. *The Need for Parties Responsible to Their Members.* Party responsibility includes also the responsibility of party leaders to the party membership, as enforced in primaries, caucuses and conventions. The external and the internal kinds of party responsibility need not conflict. Intraparty conflict will be minimized if it is generally recognized that national, state and local party leaders have a common responsibility to the party membership. National party leaders have a legitimate interest in the nomination of congressional candidates.

3. The Inadequacy of the Existing Party System

I. Beginning Transition

1. *Change and Self-Examination.* Marked changes in the structure and processes of American society have necessarily affected the party system. The prevailing climate of self-examination as well as the current tendencies toward change in the party system give point to inquiries like that represented by our report.
2. *Burden of the Past.* Formal party organization in its main features is still substantially what it was before the Civil War. Under these circumstances the main trends of American politics have tended to outflank the party system.

II. Some Basic Problems

1. *The Federal Basis.* The two parties are organized on a federal basis. The national and state party organizations are largely independent of one another, without appreciable common approach to problems of party policy and strategy. The real issue is not over the federal form of organization but over the right balance of forces within this type of organization. A corollary of the kind of federalism now expressed in the party system is an excessive measure of internal separatism.
2. *The Location of Leadership.* Party organization does not vest leadership of the party as a whole in either a single person or a committee. There is at present no central figure or organ which could claim authority to take up party problems, policies and strategy.
3. *The Ambiguity of Membership.* No understandings or rules or criteria exist with respect to membership in a party. Those who suggest that elections should deal with personalities but not with programs suggest at the same time that party membership should mean nothing at all.

III. Specific Deficiencies

1. *National Party Organs.* The National Convention, as at present constituted and operated, is an unwieldy, unrepresentative and less than responsible body. The National Committee is seldom a generally influential body and much less a working body. House and Senate campaign committees do not always have a good working relationship with the National Committee. Although interest in questions of party policy has grown, the national party organs are not so constituted nor so coordinated as to make it simple for them to pay enough attention to these questions.

2. *Party Platforms.* Alternatives between the parties are defined so badly that it is often difficult to determine what the election has decided even in broadest terms. The prevailing procedure for the writing and adoption of national party platforms is too hurried and too remote from the process by which actual decisions are made to command the respect of the whole party and the electorate. The platform should be the end product of a long search for a working agreement within the party.

3. *Intraparty Democracy.* Too little consideration has been given to ways and means of bringing about a constructive relationship between the party and its members. In making the most of popular participation, the performance of American parties is very unsatisfactory.

4. *Party Research.* A party stands as much in need of research as does business enterprise or the government itself.

4. New Demands upon Party Leadership

I. The Nature of Modern Public Policy

1. *Broad Range of Policy.* The expanding responsibilities of modern government have brought about so extensive an interlacing of governmental action with the country's economic and social life that the need for coordinated and coherent programs, legislative as well as administrative, has become paramount. In a democracy no general program can be adopted and carried out without wide public support.

2. *Impact on the Public.* In a predominantly industrial society, public policy tends to be widely inclusive, involving in its objectives and effects very large segments of the public or even the whole country.

3. *Governmental Program Machinery.* On the side of government, in the administrative and the legislative spheres, the twin needs for program formulation and for program machinery have long been recognized. The governmental advance toward program formulation needs now to be paralleled in the political sphere proper above all, in the party system.

II. Rise of Nation-wide Policy Issues

1. *An Historic Trend.* The changes in the nature and scope of public policy are the result of changes in the social structure and in the economy of the United States.
2. *Past and Present Factors.* There has been in recent decades a continuing decline of sectionalism. Party organization designed to deal with the increasing volume of national issues must give wide range to the national party leadership.
3. *New Interest Groups in Politics.* The economic and social factors that have reduced the weight of sectionalism have also resulted in the development of a new type of interest groups, built upon large membership. To a much greater extent than in the past, they operate as if they were auxiliary organizations of one or the other party.

5. *The Question of Constitutional Amendment*

1. *A Cabinet System?* A responsible cabinet system makes the leaders of the majority collectively accountable for the conduct of the government.
2. *Strong Parties as a Condition.* To amend the Constitution in order to create a responsible cabinet system is not a practicable way of getting more effective parties.
3. *Adaptation within the Constitution.* The parties can do much to adapt the usages under the Constitution to their purposes.

PART II. PROPOSALS FOR PARTY RESPONSIBIUTY

6. *National Party Organization*

I. Principal Party Bodies

1. *The National Convention.* We assume its continuation as the principal representative and deliberative organ of the party. The convention should meet at least biennially, with easy provision for special meetings. It should also cease to be a delegate convention of unwieldy size.
2. *The National Committee.* It is highly desirable for the National Convention to reassert its authority over the National Committee through a more active participation in the final selection of the committee membership. It is also desirable that the members of the National Committee reflect the actual strength of the party within the areas they represent.

3.   *The Party Council.* We propose a Party Council of 50 members. Such
a Party Council should consider and settle the larger problems of party
management, within limits prescribed by the National Convention;
propose a preliminary draft of the party platform to the National
Convention; interpret the platform in relation to current problems;
choose for the National Convention the group of party leaders outside
the party organizations; consider and make recommendations to
appropriate party organs in respect to congressional candidates; and
make recommendations to the National Convention, the National
Committee or other appropriate party organs with respect to conspicuous departures from general party decisions by state or local party
organizations. In presidential years, the council would naturally
become a place for the discussion of presidential candidacies, and might
well perform the useful function of screening these candidacies in a
preliminary way. Within this Party Council there might well be a
smaller group of party advisers to serve as a party cabinet.

II. Intraparty Relationships

1.   *State and Local Party Organizations.* Organizational patterns of the
parties are predicated on the assumption that a party committee is
necessary for each electoral area. There is a growing dissatisfaction
with the results of this system on the local level, especially the
multiplicity of organizations. An increasing number of state legislators
are noting the breakdown or lack of party responsibility and discipline
and the growth of internal separatism in state government. It is
necessary for both parties to reexamine their purposes and functions
in the light of the present-day environment, state and local, in which
they operate.

2.   *Relations between National, State and Local Organizations.* Establish-
ment of a Party Council would do much to coordinate the different
party organizations, and should be pressed with that objective in
mind. Regional conferences held by both parties have clearly been
fruitful. Regional party organizations should be encouraged. Local
party organizations should be imbued with a stronger sense of loyalty
to the entire party organization and feel their responsibility for
promoting the broader policies of the party. This can be done by
fostering local party meetings, regularly and frequently held, perhaps
monthly. The national organization may deal with conspicuous or
continued disloyalty on the part of any state organization. Consideration should be given to the development of additional means of dealing
with rebellious and disloyal state organizations.

3.   *Headquarters and Staff.* Both parties are now aware of the need to
maintain permanent headquarters, with staff equipped for research and

publicity. A beginning has been made, but much still remains to be done. Staff development at party headquarters provides the essential mechanism to enable each party to concern itself appropriately with its continuing responsibilities.

7. *Party Platforms*

I. Nature of the Platform

1. *Alternative Purposes.* Should the party platform be a statement of general principles representing the permanent or long-range philosophy of the party? Or should it state the party's position on immediate issues? Actually, the platform is usually made up of both the more permanent and the more fleeting elements.
2. *Interpretation of the Platform.* As a body representing the various parts of the party structure, the Party Council should be able to give authoritative and reasonably acceptable interpretations of the platform.
3. *National-State Platform Conflicts.* What is needed is better coordination in the declaration of party principles. The Party Council would be the appropriate party agency to interpret the respective platforms and determine the right position in ease of conflict. There is very little likelihood indeed for the Party Council to be inconsiderate of arguable claims of state autonomy.
4. *Binding Character.* In spite of clear implications and express pledges, there has been much difference of opinion as to the exact binding quality of a platform. All of this suggests the need for appropriate machinery, such as a Party Council, to interpret and apply the national program in respect to doubts or details. When that is done by way of authoritative and continuing statement, the party program should be considered generally binding.

II. Problems of Platform-Making

1. *Method of Formulating Party Platforms.* Occasionally the state platforms are deliberately delayed until after the national platform bas been adopted, in order to have a basis for conformity. Such practice is to be encouraged, and state legislation that prevents it ought to be changed. A method of platform-making that is closely related to the congressional as well as to the presidential campaign must be developed, and with more direct participation by the party members of Congress.
2. *Improvement of Platforms and Platform-Making.* In both parties, the Platform Committee or a working part of it is now appointed some weeks in advance of the National Convention. The practice of holding

public hearings on the policies to be incorporated into the platform has been fairly well established. This consultation is of importance, for it makes the parties aware of the interest in particular policies.

3. *Proposals.* Party platforms should be formulated at least every two years. National platforms should emphasize general party principles and national issues. State and local platforms should be expected to conform to the national platform on matters of general party principle or on national policies. To achieve better machinery for platform-making, the Party Council, when set up, should prepare a tentative draft well in advance of the National Convention for the consideration of the appropriate convention committee and the convention itself. Local party meetings should be held for the discussion and consideration of platform proposals.

8. Party Organization in Congress

I. Introduction

1. *External Factors.* A higher degree of party responsibility in Congress cannot be provided merely by actions taken within Congress. Nevertheless, action within Congress can be of decisive significance.
2. *Continuous Evolution.* The materials for responsible party operations in Congress are already on hand. The key to progress lies in making a full-scale effort to use them.

II. Tightening Up the Congressional Party Organization

1. *The Leaders.* For more than ten years now the press has carried news about regular meetings between the President and the Big Four of Congress—the Speaker of the House, the Majority Leader of the House, the Vice-President and the Majority Leader of the Senate, when the four are of the President's party. It would be an error to attempt to supplant the relationship between the Big Four and the President by some new body. Whenever it becomes necessary for the President to meet with the leaders of both parties in Congress, it is a simple matter for the Big Four to be expanded to six or eight. In the public eye a party leader like these is a spokesman for his party as a whole. It is necessary that there be broad consultation throughout the national leadership of a party before a party leader is elected in either house.
2. *The Leadership Committees.* We submit these proposals: In both the Senate and the House, the various leadership groups should be consolidated into one truly effective and responsible leadership committee for each party. Each of these four committees should be responsible not only for submitting policy proposals to the party

membership, but also for discharging certain functions with respect to the committee structure and the legislative schedule. Each of the four committees should be selected or come up for a vote of confidence no less often than every two years. Occasion must be found reasonably often for the leadership committees of each party in the two houses to meet together. Furthermore, the rival leadership committees in each house should meet together on a more regular basis. A case can also be made for the four leadership groups to meet on specific occasions.

3. *Caucuses or Conferences.* More frequent meetings of the party membership in each house should be held. A binding caucus decision on legislative policy should be used primarily to carry out the party's principles and program. When members of Congress disregard a caucus decision taken in furtherance of national party policy, they should expect disapproval. The party leadership committees should be responsible for calling more frequent caucuses or conferences and developing the agenda of points for discussion.

III. Party Responsibility for Committee Structure

1. *Selection of Committee Chairmen.* It is not playing the game fairly for party members who oppose the commitments in their party's platform to rely on seniority to carry them into committee chairmanships. Party leaders have compelling reason to prevent such a member from becoming chairman and they are entirely free so to exert their influence. The task of party leaders, when confronted with revolt on the part of committee chairmen, is not easy. Obviously problems of this sort must be handled in the electoral process itself as well as in the congressional arena.

2. *Assignment of Members Committees.* The slates of committee assignments should be drawn up by the party leadership committees and presented to the appropriate party caucuses for approval or modification. There is nothing sound in having the party ratio on the committees always correspond closely to the party ratio in the House itself. Committee assignments should be subjected to regular reexamination by the party caucus or conference with reasonable frequency.

3. *Committee Staff.* Staff assistance should be available to minority as well as majority members of a committee whenever they want it. Where all committee staff is controlled by the majority, a change in power threatens continuity of service.

IV. Party Responsibility for the Legislative Schedule

1. *The Need for Scheduling.* Schedules should be openly explained on the floor in advance. No committee should be in charge of legislative scheduling except the party leadership committee.

2. *House Guidance of Legislative Traffic.* A democratic approach would be to substitute open party control for control by the Rules Committee or individual chairmen.

3. *The Right to Vote in the Senate.* The present cloture rule should be amended. The best rule is one that provides for majority cloture on all matters before the Senate.

9. Political Participation

Widespread political participation fosters responsibility as well as democratic control in the conduct of party affairs and the pursuit of party policies. A more responsible party system is intimately linked with the general level as well as the forms of political participation.

I. Intraparty Democracy

1. *Party Membership.* As stress is placed by the parties upon policy and the interrelationship of problems at various levels of government, association with a party should become more interesting and attractive to many who hold aloof today.

2. *Machinery of Intraparty Democracy.* If the National Convention is to serve as the grand assembly of the party, in which diverse viewpoints are compounded into a course of action, it must be nourished from below. To this end local party groups are needed that meet frequently to discuss and initiate policy.

3. *Toward a New Concept of Party Membership.* The existence of a national program, drafted at frequent intervals by a party convention both broadly representative and enjoying prestige, should make a great difference. It would prompt those who identify themselves as Republicans or Democrats to think in terms of support of that program, rather than in terms of personalities, patronage and local matters. Once machinery is established which gives the party member and his representative a share in framing the party's objectives, once there are safeguards against internal dictation by a few in positions of influence, members and representatives will feel readier to assume an obligation to support the program. Membership defined in these terms does not ask for mindless discipline enforced from above. It generates self-discipline which stems from free identification with aims one helps to define.

II. Nominating Procedure

1. *United States Senator and Representative.* Nominations for United States Senator and Representative are governed largely by state laws that vary radically in their provisions. National regulation would

overcome the disadvantages of so much variety. But one must face the practical objections to national regulation. The direct primary probably can be adapted to the needs of parties unified in terms of national policy. The closed primary deserves preference because it is more readily compatible with the development of a responsible party system. The open primary tends to destroy the concept of membership as the basis of party organization. Cross filing is bound to obscure program differences between the parties, and to eliminate any sense of real membership on the part of the rank and file. The Washington blanket primary corrupts the meaning of party even further by permitting voters at the same primary to roam at will among the parties. The formal or informal proposal of candidates by preprimary meetings of responsible party committees or party councils is a healthy development. Quite appropriately the Party Council might become a testing ground for candidates for United States Senator or Representative.

2. *Presidential Nomination.* In the National Convention, delegates representative of the party membership should be chosen by direct vote of the rank and file. The Party Council naturally would concern itself with platform plans and the relative claims of those who might be considered for presidential and vice-presidential nominations. In time it may be feasible and desirable to substitute a direct, national presidential primary for the indirect procedure of the convention.

III. Elections

1. *Election of the President.* The present method of electing the President and Vice President fosters the blight of one-party monopoly and results in concentration of campaign artillery in pivotal industrial states where minority groups hold the balance of power. In the persistent agitation for change in the Electoral College system, stress should be placed both upon giving all sections of the country a real voice in electing the President and the Vice President and upon developing a two-party system in present one-party areas.

2. *Term of Representative.* It appears desirable to lengthen the term of Representatives to four years.

3. *Campaign Funds.* Existing statutory limitations work toward a scattering of responsibility for the collecting of funds among a large number of independent party and nonparty committees. Repeal of these restrictions would make it possible for a national body to assume more responsibility in the field of party finance. The situation might be improved in still another way by giving a specified measure of government assistance to the parties. Everything that makes the party system more meaningful to all voters leads incidentally to a broadening of the base of financial support of the parties.

4. *Apportionment and Redistricting.* It is time to insist upon congressional districts approximately equal in population.

IV. Barriers to Voting

1. *Registration.* The system of permanent registration should be extended. Properly qualified newcomers to an area should be permitted to register to vote without undue delay.
2. *Access to the Polls.* Legislation establishing National Election Day would in all probability bring to the polls large numbers of people who would otherwise never come. Holding elections on Saturdays or Sundays would probably also help to increase the size of the vote. Adequate voting time should be provided by opening the booths in the earlier morning hours and keeping them open into the late evening hours. There is room for much elaboration in laws governing absentee balloting.
3. *Undemocratic Limitations.* Intentionally limiting devices should be overcome by a combination of legal change and educational efforts. Action is indicated to extend the suffrage to the inhabitants of the District of Columbia.
4. *The Short Ballot.* Adoption of the short ballot would concentrate choice on contests with program implications and thus shift attention toward issues rather than personalities.

10. Research on Political Parties

I. Basic Facts and Figures

1. *Election Statistics.* We propose the publication of an election yearbook by the Bureau of the Census. The arrangement of the yearbook should probably be by states. In addition, a summary booklet for presidential and congressional elections should be issued.
2. *Party Activities.* Compilation and regular publication of information on party activities are no less urgently needed.
3. *Compilation of Party Regulations.* A third task is the collection of all major regulations relating to national parties and elections.

II. More Research by the Parties

1. *Party Research Staffs.* What is needed is a stronger full-time research organization adequately financed and working on a year-in, year-out basis.
2. *Areas of Work.* There are two fields of research that should always be of immediate interest to the national organization of every party.

The first is the analysis of voting trends and voting behavior. A second research field is analysis of proposals dealing with changes in election methods.

III. More Studies of the Parties

1. *Types of Research Needed.* In a field in which much still remains to be done, specific priorities have little meaning. The basic need is for a combination of creative hypotheses and realistic investigations.
2. *Professors and Politics.* The character of political research cannot be dissociated from the general approach of academic institutions to politics as a whole. Increased faculty participation in political affairs would mean more practical, realistic and useful teaching as well as research in the field of political parties.
3. *Role of Research Foundations.* The private foundations should actively solicit new ideas and proposals for research on political parties.
4. *Role of American Political Science Association.* The presentation of this report is but one instance of the interest shown in the subject of political parties by the American Political Science Association. In making specific suggestions in this field, the Association could exert a further welcome influence.

PART III. THE PROSPECT FOR ACTION

11. Sources of Support and Leadership

Readjustments in the structure and operation of the political parties call for a widespread appreciation, by influential parts of the public as well as by political leaders and party officials, of the kinds of change that are needed in order to bring about a more responsible operation of the two-party system.

1. *The Economic Pressure Groups.* Highly organized special interests with small or no direct voting power are best satisfied if the individual legislator and administrative officials are kept defenseless in the face of their special pressure. Organizations with large membership are not in the same category. It is reasonable to expect that those large-membership organizations with wise leadership will generally support the turn toward more responsible parties.
2. *The Party Leaders.* Leaders who represent divergent sectional or other special interests within each party will look with disfavor upon any reforms that hit specifically at their personal vested interests. Most of the forward-looking leaders in each party are convinced that changes should be made.

3. *The Government Officialdom.* Greater program responsibility at the level of the political parties is likely to appeal to administrators and the career officialdom.
4. *Congress.* It cannot be expected that all congressional leaders will be sympathetic to the concept of party responsibility. As leaders of national opinion, influential members of each party in Congress can give strong support to the idea of party responsibility.
5. *The President.* The President can probably be more influential than any other single individual in attaining a better organized majority party, and thus also prompting the minority party to follow suit. With greater party responsibility, the President's position as party leader would correspond in strength to the greater strength of his party.
6. *The Electorate.* The electorate consists of three main groups: (1) those who seldom or never vote; (2) those who vote regularly for the party of their traditional affiliation; and (3) those who base their electoral choice upon the political performance of the two parties, as indicated by the programs they support and the candidates they succeed in putting forward. The rank and file in each party want their party so organized that the views of the party majority will be respected and carried out. It may well be the members of the third group who, in making their choices at election time, will decide the question of our country's progress in the direction of a more responsible party system. It is this group that occupies a place of critical importance in supporting a party system able to shoulder national responsibility.

12. The Dangers of Inaction

Four dangers warrant special emphasis. The first danger is that the inadequacy of the party system in sustaining well-considered programs and providing broad public support for them may lead to grave consequences in an explosive era. The second danger is that the American people may go too far for the safety of constitutional government in compensating for this inadequacy by shifting excessive responsibility to the President. The third danger is that with growing public cynicism and continuing proof of the ineffectiveness of the party system the nation may eventually witness the disintegration of the two major parties. The fourth danger is that the incapacity of the two parties for consistent action based on meaningful programs may rally support for extremist parties poles apart, each fanatically bent on imposing on the country its particular panacea.

1. *The Danger of an Explosive Era.* The political foundation of appropriate governmental programs is very unstable when it is not supplied by responsible party action.
2. *The Danger of Overextending the Presidency.* Dependable political support has to be built up for the governmental program. When there

is no other place to get that done, when the political parties fail to do it, it is tempting to turn to the President. When the President's program actually is the sole program, either his party becomes a flock of sheep or the party falls apart, This concept of the presidency disposes of the party system by making the President reach directly for the support of a majority of the voters.

3. *The Danger of Disintegration of the Two Parties.* A chance that the electorate will turn its back upon the two parties is by no means academic. As a matter of fact, this development has already occurred in considerable part, and it is still going on. American political institutions are too firmly grounded upon the two-party system to make its collapse a small matter.

4. *The Danger of an Unbridgeable Political Cleavage.* If the two parties do not develop alternative programs that can be executed, the voter's frustration and the mounting ambiguities of national policy might set in motion more extreme tendencies to the political left and the political right. Once a deep political cleavage develops between opposing groups, each group naturally works to keep it deep. Orientation of the American two-party system along the lines of meaningful national programs is a significant step toward avoiding the development of such a cleavage.

Note

1. From the *American Political Science Review*, 44, II (September 1950), pp. 1–14. With permission from the American Political Science Association.

Appendix B
Data for Exercises 4.1, 4.2, 4.3, and 5.2

Country	Partyname	Struc-tartic	Natof-struct	Area	Popu-lation	Feder-alism	Pres-parl	Cohes-ion
USA	Democrat	2.00	1.00	2.00	2.00	2.00	1.00	1.00
USA	Republicans	2.00	1.00	2.00	2.00	2.00	1.00	1.00
UK	Labour	2.00	2.00	2.00	2.00	1.00	2.00	2.00
UK	Conservatives	2.00	2.00	2.00	2.00	1.00	2.00	2.00
Australia	Labour	1.00	1.00	2.00	2.00	2.00	2.00	2.00
Australia	Liberal	2.00	1.00	2.00	2.00	2.00	2.00	2.00
Australia	Country	1.00	1.00	2.00	2.00	2.00	2.00	2.00
Canada	Progressive-Conservative	2.00	1.00	2.00	2.00	2.00	2.00	2.00
Canada	Liberal	2.00	1.00	2.00	2.00	2.00	2.00	2.00
Canada	New Democratic	2.00	2.00	2.00	2.00	2.00	2.00	2.00
Canada	Social Credit	1.00	1.00	2.00	2.00	2.00	2.00	
New Zealand	National	2.00	1.00	2.00	1.00	1.00	2.00	2.00
New Zealand	Labour	2.00	1.00	2.00	1.00	1.00	2.00	2.00
Ireland	Fianna Fail	1.00	2.00	1.00	1.00	1.00	2.00	2.00
Ireland	Fine Gael	1.00	2.00	1.00	1.00	1.00	2.00	2.00
Ireland	Irish Labour	1.00	2.00	1.00	1.00	1.00	2.00	2.00
India	National Congress	2.00	2.00	2.00	2.00	2.00	2.00	2.00
India	Communist	2.00	2.00	2.00	2.00	2.00	2.00	2.00
Austria	Austrian People's	2.00	1.00	1.00	2.00	1.00	2.00	2.00
Austria	Austrian Socialist	2.00	2.00	1.00	2.00	1.00	2.00	2.00
Austria	Liberal	1.00	1.00	1.00	2.00	1.00	2.00	1.00
France	Fr Popular Republican Movement	2.00	1.00	2.00	2.00	1.00	2.00	1.00
France	Fr Radical Socialist	1.00	1.00	2.00	2.00	1.00	2.00	1.00
France	Fr Socialist Party	2.00	2.00	2.00	2.00	1.00	2.00	2.00
France	Gaullist	1.00	2.00	2.00	2.00	1.00	2.00	1.00
France	Fr Communist	2.00	2.00	2.00	2.00	1.00	2.00	2.00
West Germany	CDU	2.00	1.00	2.00	2.00	2.00	2.00	1.00
West Germany	Social Democratic	2.00	2.00	2.00	2.00	2.00	2.00	2.00
West Germany	Free Democrats	1.00	1.00	2.00	2.00	2.00	2.00	1.00
Greece	Liberal	1.00	2.00	1.00	2.00	1.00	2.00	

continued . . .

Continued

Country	Partyname	Struc-tartic	Natof-struct	Area	Popu-lation	Feder-alism	Pres-parl	Cohes-ion
Greece	National Progressive Union of the Center	1.00		1.00	2.00	1.00	2.00	
Greece	National Radical Union	1.00	2.00	1.00	2.00	1.00	2.00	2.00
Greece	United Democratic Left	2.00	2.00	1.00	2.00	1.00	2.00	
Denmark	Social Democratic	2.00	2.00	1.00	1.00	1.00	2.00	2.00
Denmark	Moderate Liberal	2.00	2.00	1.00	1.00	1.00	2.00	2.00
Denmark	Conservative Peoples	2.00	2.00	1.00	1.00	1.00	2.00	2.00
Denmark	Radical Left	2.00	2.00	1.00	1.00	1.00	2.00	2.00
Iceland	Independence	1.00	2.00	1.00	1.00	1.00	2.00	
Iceland	Progressive	1.00	2.00	1.00	1.00	1.00	2.00	
Iceland	People's Union	1.00	2.00	1.00	1.00	1.00	2.00	
Iceland	Social Democratic	1.00		1.00	1.00	1.00	2.00	
Sweden	Social Democratic Labour	2.00	1.00	2.00	2.00	1.00	2.00	2.00
Sweden	Agrarian	2.00	1.00	2.00	2.00	1.00	2.00	2.00
Sweden	People's	2.00	1.00	2.00	2.00	1.00	2.00	1.00
Sweden	Swedish Right	2.00	1.00	2.00	2.00	1.00	2.00	1.00
Netherlands	Catholic People's	2.00	2.00	1.00	2.00	1.00	2.00	2.00
Netherlands	Labour	2.00	2.00	1.00	2.00	1.00	2.00	2.00
Netherlands	Liberal		1.00	1.00	2.00	1.00	2.00	2.00
Netherlands	Anti-Revolutionary	2.00	2.00	1.00	2.00	1.00	2.00	2.00
Netherlands	Christian Historical Union	1.00	1.00	1.00	2.00	1.00	2.00	1.00
Netherlands	Communist	2.00	2.00	1.00	2.00	1.00	2.00	2.00
Luxembourg	Christian Social Union	1.00	2.00	1.00	1.00	1.00	2.00	2.00
Luxembourg	Socialist Labour	2.00		1.00	1.00	1.00	2.00	
Luxembourg	Liberal	2.00	2.00	1.00	1.00	1.00	2.00	
Luxembourg	Communist	2.00		1.00	1.00	1.00	2.00	2.00
Ecuador	National Velasquista Federation	1.00		2.00	1.00	1.00	2.00	
Ecuador	Conservative	1.00	2.00	2.00	1.00	1.00	2.00	
Ecuador	Radical Liberal	1.00	2.00	2.00	1.00	1.00	2.00	
Ecuador	Socialist	1.00		2.00	1.00	1.00	2.00	
Ecuador	Ecuadorian Concentration of Popular Forces	1.00		2.00	1.00	1.00	2.00	
Peru	National Union	1.00		2.00	2.00	1.00	1.00	2.00
Peru	Christian Democratic	1.00		2.00	2.00	1.00	1.00	2.00
Peru	American Popular Revolutionary Alliance	1.00	2.00	2.00	2.00	1.00	1.00	2.00

continued . . .

Continued

Country	Partyname	Struc-tartic	Natof-struct	Area	Popu-lation	Feder-alism	Pres-parl	Cohes-ion
Peru	Popular Action	2.00	2.00	2.00	2.00	1.00	1.00	1.00
Peru	Peruvian Democratic Movement	1.00		2.00	2.00	1.00	1.00	1.00
Uruguay	Colorados	2.00	1.00	1.00	1.00	1.00	1.00	1.00
Uruguay	Blancos	2.00	1.00	1.00	1.00	1.00	1.00	1.00
Venezuela	Democratic Republican Union	1.00	1.00	2.00	1.00	1.00	2.00	
Venezuela	Social Christian	1.00	2.00	2.00	1.00	1.00	2.00	2.00
Venezuela	Democratic Action	2.00	2.00	2.00	1.00	1.00	2.00	
Guatemala	National Democratic Union		1.00	1.00	1.00	1.00		
Guatemala	Christian Democratic	1.00		1.00	1.00	1.00	1.00	1.00
Guatemala	Revolutionary	1.00	2.00	1.00	1.00	1.00	1.00	1.00
Guatemala	National Democratic Reconcil		1.00	1.00	1.00	1.00		
Burma	Anti-Fascist People's Freedom	1.00	2.00	2.00	2.00	1.00	2.00	1.00
Burma	Stable Anti-Fascist People's Freedom	1.00	2.00	2.00	2.00	1.00	2.00	2.00
Burma	Clean Anti-Fascist People's Freedom	1.00	2.00	2.00	2.00	1.00	2.00	1.00
Malaya	United Malayan National Organization	1.00	2.00	1.00	1.00	1.00	2.00	2.00
Malaya	Malayan Chinese Association	1.00	2.00	1.00	1.00	1.00	2.00	2.00
Malaya	Malayan Indian Congress	1.00	2.00	1.00	1.00	1.00	2.00	2.00
Malaya	Pan-Malayan Islamic Party	1.00	2.00	1.00	1.00	1.00	2.00	2.00
Lebanon	Progressive Socialist	2.00	2.00	1.00	1.00	1.00	2.00	2.00
Lebanon	Lebanese Constitutionalist Bloc	1.00	1.00	1.00	1.00	1.00	2.00	2.00
Lebanon	Lebanese Phalanges	2.00	2.00	1.00	1.00	1.00	2.00	2.00
Lebanon	Lebanese Nationalist Bloc	1.001	2.00	1.00	1.00	1.00	2.00	
Dahomey	Nationalist	1.00	2.00	1.00	1.00	1.00	2.00	
Dahomey	Democratic Union	1.00	2.00	1.00	1.00	1.00	2.00	
Dahomey	Democratic Rally	2.00	2.00	1.00	1.00	1.00	2.00	
Kenya	African National Union	2.00	1.00	2.00	1.00	1.00	2.00	
Kenya	African Democratic Union	2.00	1.00	2.00	1.00	1.00	2.00	
Turkey	Republican People's	2.00	2.00	2.00	2.00	1.00	2.00	2.00
Turkey	Democratic	2.00	2.00	2.00	2.00	1.00	2.00	2.00
Uganda	People's Congress	1.00	1.00	2.00	1.00	2.00	2.00	
Uganda	Democratic	1.00	1.00	2.00	1.00	2.00	2.00	2.00
Uganda	Ugandan King Only	1.00	2.00	2.00	1.00	2.00	2.00	

Appendix C
Information for Exercise 5.1

CQ Almanac "Top Opposers of Own Party's Majority," 10-Year Increments, 1950–2010

Rank	1950—81st Congress (House) Democratic Party			1960—86th Congress (House) Democratic Party			1970—91st Congress (House) Democratic Party			1980—96th Congress (House) Democratic Party		
	Congressman	State	% Opp.	Congressman	State	% Opp.	Congressman	State	% Opp.	Congressman	State	% Opp.
1	Wheeler	GA	63	Haley	FL	73	Marsh	VA	79	McDonald	GA	87
2	Pickett	TX	62	Dorn	SC	67	Daniel	VA	74	Stump	AZ	82
3	Fisher	TX	61	Abbitt	VA	67	Satterfield	VA	72	Satterfield	VA	77
4	Wood	GA	58	Murray	TN	67	Haley	FL	65	Gramm	TX	71
5	Colmer	MS	58	Winstead	MS	67	Montgomery	MS	65	Stenholm	TX	71
6	Smith	VA	58	Brock	NE	67	Fountain	NC	64	Daniel	VA	70
7	Lucas	TX	58	Ashmore	SC	63	Abernethy	MS	64	Montgomery	MS	68
8	Stanley	VA	57	Colmer	MS	63	Brinkley	GA	63	Jacobs	IN	66
9	Wilson	TX	56	Davis	GA	63	Colmer	MS	63	Hall	TX	65
10	Davis	GA	55	Flynt	GA	61	Burleson	TX	62	Leath	TX	65
11	Abernethy	MS	55	Williams	MS	61	Bennett	FL	61	Evans	IN	62
12	Rankin	MS	55	Tuck	VA	59	Rogers	FL	60	Shelby	AL	59
13	Whitten	MS	55	Smith	VA	58	Rarick	LA	60	Ichord	MO	57
14	Secrest	OH	55	Gary	VA	56	Fisher	TX	57	Applegate	OH	55
15	Rivers	SC	55	Whitten	MS	52	Chappell	FL	57	Byron	MD	53
16	Winstead	MS	54	Harrison	VA	48	Hagan	GA	57	English	OK	53
17	Teague	TX	53	Abernethy	MS	46	Dorn	MS	56	Nichols	AL	52
18	Williams	MS	52	Dowdy	TX	45	Flowers	AL	56	Jenkins	GA	52
19	Harrison	VA	49	Kitchen	NC	44	Griffin	MS	56	Bouguard	TN	52
20	Passman	LA	49	Forrester	GA	42	Jarman	OK	56	Fountain	NC	50

CQ Almanac "Top Opposers of Own Party's Majority," 10-Year Increments, 1950–2010

	1990—101st Congress (House) Democratic Party			2000—106th Congress (House) Democratic Party			2010—111th Congress (House) Democratic Party		
Rank	Congressman	State	% Opp.	Congressman	State	% Opp.	Congressman	State	% Opp.
1	Stenholm	TX	47	Traficant	OH	78	Bright	AL	67
2	Parker	MS	46	Hall	TX	65	Taylor	MS	58
3	Hutto	FL	44	Shows	MS	49	Minnick	ID	56
4	Taylor	MS	43	Lucas	KY	46	Mitchell	AZ	53
5	Hall	TX	41	Taylor	MS	43	Childers	MS	47
6	Jacobs	IN	41	Stenholm	TX	41	Nye	VA	45
7	Hubbard	KY	40	Peterson	MN	40	Shuler	NC	40
8	Tauzin	LA	40	Barcia	MI	39	Giffords	AZ	40
9	Huckaby	LA	40	Danner	MO	39	Kratovil	MD	35
10	English	OK	38	McIntyre	NC	39	Kirkpatrick	AZ	34
11	Sarpalius	TX	38	Sisisky	VA	39	Adler	NJ	31
12	Montgomery	MS	37	Pickett	VA	36	Boren	OK	31
13	Barnard	GA	37	John	LA	35	McIntyre	NC	30
14	Ray	GA	37	Bishop	GA	35	Herseth-Sandlin	SD	29
15	Byron	MD	35	Cramer	AL	34	Marshall	GA	28
16	Penny	MN	33	Berry	AR	33	Donnelly	IN	27
17	Patterson	SC	33	Boyd	FL	32	Hill	IN	26
18	Laughlin	TX	33	Roemer	IN	31	Ellsworth	IN	24
19	Tallon	SC	31	Boswell	IA	31	Kirk	IL	23
20	Bennett	FL	31	Mollohan	WV	30	Altmire	PA	23

References

American Political Science Association (APSA). 1950. "Toward a More Responsible Two-Party System: A Report of the Committee on Political Parties." *American Political Science Review* 44(3).

"America's Political Parties: The Republican Party 1960–1992." 1996. Video. Kulture Video.

Appelbome, Peter. 2008. "With GOP Congressman's Loss, a Moderate Tradition Ends in New England." *New York Times*. November 5. Available online at: www.nytimes.com/2008/11/06/nyregion/06towns.html?_r=0 (accessed July 30, 2015).

Blondel, Jean. 1969. *An Introduction to Comparative Government*. New York: Praeger.

Blondel, Jean. 1978. *Political Parties*. London: Whitewood House.

Bond, Jon R. and Kevin B. Smith. 2016. *Analyzing American Democracy: Politics and Political Science*. 2nd ed. New York: Routledge.

Brady, David. 2014. "Sure, Congress Is Polarized. But Other Legislatures Are More So." *Washington Post*. February 17. Available online at: www.washingtonpost.com/blogs/monkey-cage/wp/2014/02/17/sure-congress-is-polarized-but-other-legislatures-are-more-so/ (accessed July 30, 2015).

Brady, David W., Joseph Cooper, and Patricia Hurley. 1979. "The Decline of Party in the U.S. House of Representatives, 1887–1968." *Legislative Studies Quarterly* 4 (August): 381–407.

Burke, Edmund. [1770] 1976. "Thoughts on the Cause of the Present Discontents." In *Edmund Burke on Government, Politics and Society*, Ed. B.W. Hill. London: Harvester.

Butler, David. 1955. "American Myths about British Parties." *Virginia Quarterly Review* 31(1): 46–56.

Carmines, Edward G. and James A. Stimson. 1980. "The Two Faces of Issue Voting." *American Political Science Review* 74(1): 78–91.

Charles, Joseph. 1961. *The Origins of the American Party System*. Williamsburg, VA: Harper Torchbook.

Chicago Tribune. 1985. "Democrat Leader Wants Miniconvention Scrapped." May 10. Available online at: http://articles.chicagotribune.com/1985-05-10/news/8501290227_1_kirk-presidential-election-party (accessed July 30, 2015).

Cillizza, Chris. 2013. "Five Reasons Why Being Speaker of the House Ain't What It Used to Be." *Washington Post*. January 3. Available online at:

www.washingtonpost.com/blogs/the-fix/wp/2013/01/03/5-reasons-why-being-speaker-of-the-house-aint-what-it-used-to-be/ (accessed July 30, 2015).

Conservative Party (United Kingdom). 1955. "United for Peace and Progress: The Conservative and Unionist Party's Policy." *Politics Resources.* Available online at: www.politicsresources.net/area/uk/man/con55.htm.

Conservative Party (United Kingdom). 1992. "The Best Future for Britain." *Politics Resources.* Available online at: www.politicsresources.net/area/uk/man/con92. htm.

Cotter, Cornelius, James L. Gibson, John F. Bibby, and Robert J. Huckshorn. 1984. *Party Organizations in American Politics.* New York: Praeger.

CQ Press. 2010. *National Party Conventions 1831–2008.* Washington, DC: CQ Press.

Crotty, William. 1977. *Political Reform and the American Experience.* New York: Thomas Y. Crowell.

De Tocqueville, Alexander. 1840 (trans. 2010) *Democracy in America.* Liberty Fund Publishing, Indianapolis. http://classiques.uqac.ca/classiques/De_tocqueville_alexis/democracy_in_america_historical_ed/democracy_in_america_vol_2.pdf (Accessed 22 January 2016)

Democratic National Committee (United States). 1952. "Democratic Party Platform of 1952." July 21. Available online at: www.presidency.ucsb.edu/ws/ ?pid=29600.

Democratic National Committee (United States). 1964. "Democratic Party Platform of 1964." August 24. Available online at: www.presidency.ucsb.edu/ ws/?pid=29603.

Democratic National Committee (United States). 1972. "Democratic Party Platform of 1972." July 10. Available online at: www.presidency.ucsb.edu/ws/ ?pid=29605.

Democratic National Committee (United States). 1974. *Charter of the Democratic Party of the United States.* Washington, DC: Democratic National Committee.

Democratic National Committee (United States). 2012. "2012 Democratic Party Platform." September 3. Available online at: www.presidency.ucsb.edu/ws/?pid= 101962.

Dennis, Jack. 1964. "Support for the Party System by the Mass Public." *American Political Science Review* 60: 600–615.

Duverger, Maurice. 1961. *Political Parties: Their Organization and Activity in the Modern State.* London: Wiley.

Duverger, Maurice. 1972. *Party Politics and Pressure Groups: A Comparative Introduction.* New York: Crowell.

Eldersveld, Samuel. 1964. *Political Parties: A Behavioral Approach.* New York: Rand McNally.

Eldersveld, Samuel. 1982. *Political Parties in American Society.* New York: Basic Books.

Epstein, Leon. 1967. *Political Parties in Western Democracies.* New York: Praeger.

Ford, Robert. 2014. "In America, Polarization Is a Problem. In Britain, It Could Be a Solution." *Washington Post.* February 20. Available online at: www. washingtonpost.com/blogs/monkey-cage/wp/2014/02/20/in-america-polarization-is-a-problem-in-britain-it-could-be-a-solution/ (accessed July 30, 2015).

Forgette, Richard. 2004. "Party Caucuses and Coordination: Assessing Caucus Activity and Party Effects." *Legislative Studies Quarterly* 29(3): 407–430.

Freeman, Jo. 2008. *We Will Be Heard: Women's Struggles for Political Power in the United States*. New York: Rowman & Littlefield.

Galston, William A. 2010. "Can a Polarized American Party System Be 'Healthy'?" *Issues in Governance Studies—Brookings*. April. Available online at: www.brookings.edu/~/media/research/files/papers/2010/4/polarization-galston/04_polarization_galston.pdf (accessed October 7, 2015).

Green, John and Paul Herrnson, Eds. 2002. *Responsible Partisanship: The Evolution of American Political Parties Since 1950*. Lawrence, KS: University of Kansas Press.

Haidt, Jonathan and Sam Abrams. 2015. "The Top 10 Reasons American Politics Are So Broken." *Washington Post Wonkblog*. January 7. Available online at: www.washingtonpost.com/news/wonkblog/wp/2015/01/07/the-top-10-reasons-american-politics-are-worse-than-ever (accessed October 7, 2015).

Harmel, Robert and Kenneth Janda. 1982. *Parties and Their Environments: Limits to Reform?* New York: Longman. Available online at: http://books.northwestern.edu/viewer.html?id=inu:inu-mntb-0006489521-bk.

Hershey, Marjorie Randon. 2013. *Party Politics in America*. New York: Pearson.

Iyengar, Shanto. 2011. *Media Politics: A Citizen's Guide*. New York: W.W. Norton & Co.

Janda, Kenneth. 1980. *Political Parties: A Cross-National Survey*. New York: Free Press. Available online at: http://janda.org/ICPP/ICPP1980/index.htm.

Janda, Kenneth, Jeffrey Berry, and Jerry Goldman. 1987. *The Challenge of Democracy*. Boston, MA: Houghton-Mifflin Company.

Katz, Richard and Peter Mair. 1992. *Party Organizations: A Data Handbook on Party Organizations in Western Democracies, 1960–90*. London: Sage.

Keefe, William. 1972. *Parties, Politics, and Public Policy in America*. New York: Holt.

Keefe, William J. and Morris S. Ogul. 2001. *The American Legislative Process: Congress and the States*. Upper Saddle River, NJ: Prentice Hall.

Kirkpatrick, Evron. 1971. "Toward a More Responsible Two-Party System: Political Science, Policy Science, or Pseudo-Science?" *American Political Science Review* 65: 965–990.

Klein, Ezra. 2015. "America's Political System Isn't Going to Collapse. It's Going to Muddle Through." *Vox*. March 4. Available online at: www.vox.com/2015/3/4/8140911/american-politics-crushing-disappointment (accessed October 7, 2015).

Labour Party (United Kingdom). 1955. "Forward with Labour: Labour's Policy for the Consideration of the Nation." *Politics Resources*. Available online at: www.politicsresources.net/area/uk/man/lab55.htm.

Labour Party (United Kingdom). 1974. "Let Us Work Together: Labour's Way Out of the Crisis." *Politics Resources*. Available online at: www.politicsresources.net/area/uk/man/lab74feb.htm.

Labour Party (United Kingdom). 1987. "Britain Will Win with Labour." *Politics Resources*. Available online at: www.politicsresources.net/area/uk/man/lab87.htm.

Layman, Geoffrey C. and Thomas M. Carsey. 2002. "Party Polarization and 'Conflict Extension' in the American Electorate." *American Journal of Political Science* 46: 786–802.

Leach, Robert, Bill Coxall, and Lynton Robins. 2011. *British Politics*. New York: Palgrave Macmillan.

Lockard, Duane. 1959. *New England State Politics*. Princeton, NJ: Princeton University Press.

Mann, Thomas E. 2014. "Admit It, Political Scientists: Politics Really Is More Broken Than Ever." *The Atlantic*. May 26. Available online at: www.theatlantic. com/politics/archive/2014/05/dysfunction/371544/ (accessed October 7, 2015).

Marx, Karl and Friedrich Engels. [1933] 1964. *The Communist Manifesto*, New York: Monthly Review Press.

McCarty, Nolan, Keith T. Poole, and Howard Rosenthal. 2008. *Polarized America: The Dance of Ideology and Unequal Riches*. Cambridge, MA: MIT Press.

Moss, David A. 2012. "Fixing What's Wrong with U.S. Politics." *Harvard Business Review*. March. Available online at: https://hbr.org/2012/03/fixing-whats-wrong-with-us-politics (accessed October 7, 2015).

Ornstein, Norman J., Thomas E. Mann, Michael J. Malbin, Andrew Rugg, and Raffaela Wakeman. 2014. *Vital Statistics on Congress*. Washington, DC: Brookings Institute.

Ozbudun, Ergun. 1970. *Party Cohesion in Western Democracies: A Causal Analysis*. Beverly Hills, CA: Sage Publications.

Paddock, Joel. 2005. *State and National Parties and American Democracy*. Bern: Peter Lang.

Progress Party (Denmark). "Progress Party Manifesto" 1989.

Ranney, Austin. 1951. "Toward a More Responsible Two-Party System: A Commentary." *American Political Science Review* 45(2): 488–499.

Reichley, James. 1992. *The Life of the Parties: A History of American Political Parties*. New York: Maxwell.

Repass, David E. 1971. "Issue Salience and Party Choice." *American Political Science Review* 65(2): 389–400.

Republican National Committee (United States). 1952. "Republican Party Platform of 1952." July 7. Available online at: www.presidency.ucsb.edu/ws/ ?pid=25837.

Republican National Committee (United States). 1992. "Republican Party Platform of 1992." August 17. Available online at: www.presidency.ucsb.edu/ ws/?pid=25847.

Republican National Committee (United States). 1988. "Republican Party Platform of 1988." August 16. Available online at: www.presidency.ucsb.edu/ ws/?pid=25846.

Republican National Committee (United States). 2008. "2008 Republican Party Platform." September 1. Available online at: www.presidency.ucsb.edu/ws/ ?pid=78545.

Republican National Committee (United States). 2012. "2012 Republican Party Platform." August 27. Available online at: www.presidency.ucsb.edu/ws/ ?pid=101961.

Rettig, Jessica. 2010. "Why Political Polarization Might be Good for America." *U.S. News and World Report*. May 27. Available online at: www.usnews.com/opinion/articles/2010/05/27/why-political-polarization-might-be-good-for-america (accessed October 7, 2015).

Schattschneider, E.E. 1942. *Party Government*. New York: Holt.

Social Democratic Party (Denmark). "Social Democratic Party Manifesto" 1961.

Social Democratic Party (Denmark). "Social Democratic Party Manifesto" 1977.

Social Democratic Party (Denmark). "Social Democratic Party Manifesto" 1980.

Stanley, Harold and Richard Niemi. 1990. *Vital Statistics on American Politics*. Washington, DC: CQ Press.

Truman, David. 1955. "Federalism and the Party System." In *Federalism: Mature and Emergent*, Ed. Arthur Macmahon. Garden City, NY: Doubleday, pp. 115–136.

Turner, Julius. 1951. "Responsible Parties: A Dissent from the Floor." *American Political Science Review* 45(1): 143–152.

Wilson, James Q. 1973. *Political Organizations*. New York: Basic Books.

Yergin, Daniel and Joseph Stanislaw. 1997. *The Commanding Heights*. New York: Simon & Schuster.

Index